Effective Schools and Effective Teachers

Gary A. Davis

University of Wisconsin—Madison

Margaret A. Thomas

*University of Wisconsin—Madison
and Beloit, Wisconsin, Public Schools*

Allyn and Bacon

Boston   London   Sydney   Toronto

To Dan Davis
    Terry Davis
    Jimmy Ellenberger

Copyright © 1989 by Allyn and Bacon
A Division of Simon & Schuster
160 Gould Street
Needham Heights, Massachusetts 02194-2310

Series Editorial Assistant: Terry Williams
Production Administrator: Annette Joseph
Production Coordinator: Susan Freese
Editorial-Production Service: Laura Cleveland
Text Design: Denise Hoffman, Glenview Studios
Cover Administrator: Linda K. Dickinson
Cover Designer: Christy Rosso
Manufacturing Buyer: Tamara McCracken

Library of Congress Cataloging-in-Publication Data
Davis, Gary A., 1938–
    Effective schools and effective teachers / Gary A. Davis, Margaret
A. Thomas
        p.   cm.
    Bibliography: p.
    Includes index.
    ISBN 0-205-11921-2
    1. School management and organization.   2. School supervision.
3. Teachers—Rating of.   I. Thomas, Margaret A.   II. Title.
LB2805.D23   1989
371.2—dc19   88-32658
                                                                            CIP

Printed in the United States of America

10 9 8 7 6 5 4 3   94 93 92

Contents

Preface

In the past two decades, research on effective schooling has addressed some basic questions: What characteristics of schools are related to higher levels of student achievement? What traits of principals contribute to school success? What teacher characteristics and classroom behaviors produce high achievement? Sensible, sometimes disarmingly logical answers have poured in, answers that have been confirmed and reconfirmed in research with poor and middle-class children in both elementary and secondary settings.

The effective-schooling movement, built entirely on research-based findings and recommendations, has had a major impact on the educational community. It has raised the school-improvement consciousness of state, district, and building administrators, who see a clearer picture of what creates a successful school where all children can learn. It has helped teachers understand how sometimes small changes in attitudes and teaching and management habits can raise the achievement level of every child. It has helped schools and colleges of education nation-wide make sound improvements in their educational administration and teacher training programs.

In fact, most states have adopted school-improvement programs that reflect findings reported in the effective-schooling literature, particularly the five core school-level characteristics of strong instructional leadership, a safe and orderly school climate, high expectations for achievement, an emphasis on basic skills, and continuous monitoring of progress (U.S. Department of Education, 1986, 1987).

This book introduces educators to the major findings of effective-schooling research. Although it was written primarily for teachers, the book also provides an overview for administrators and others who are interested in the subject. The principles and recommendations can help teachers understand attitudes and expectations, teaching and reviewing strategies, and classroom management tactics that promote interest and raise achievement, as well as those that work against successful teaching. Without knowledge of these carefully identified and confirmed principles, it is possible to spend a professional lifetime discovering the hard way how to become a good teacher—one who is successful, reflective, respected, and well liked.

The book includes a description of the characteristics, behaviors, and school-improvement strategies of effective principals, considered by many to be the single most essential ingredient for school improvement and success. It is desirable for teachers and other staff to understand the orientation and activities of effective school administrators, just as it is desirable for administrators to understand what research says about characteristics of effective classroom teachers.

The effective-schooling research includes four main topics: characteristics of effective schools, characteristics of effective principals, characteristics of effective teachers, and effective classroom management. These topics are covered in Chapters 2 through 5. The four topics are interrelated and overlapping. For example, such central features as creating an academic climate and optimizing students' time on task appear in the research literature on all four topics. Chapter 6 supplements them with a discussion of the principal-teacher observation and supervision process and strategies for teacher collaboration to improve teaching.

The topic of characteristics of effective schooling inherently demands lists of these characteristics. Every major research study or literature review, in fact, has produced such a list. While lists of ideas may create tedious reading, the information contained in them justifies a thoughtful examination.

The book is heavily documented; in fact, in places it may resemble a professional journal. The purpose of the documentation is both to emphasize the research base underlying virtually all of the recommendations and to provide specific resources for further reading.

We are well aware that the findings and recommendations are presented in an oversimplified fashion. The uniqueness of each school, its student body composition, its community values and expectations, and the uniqueness of each principal, classroom, teacher, subject area, and individual student adds complexities that may influence the suitability of any recommendation. Furthermore, many critics have put the effective-schooling research under a microscope to stress its weaknesses and shortcomings. For example, results of different studies have not produced exactly the same results; results from lower-class schools may not apply to middle-class schools; the focus on reading and mathematics achievement is short-sighted; the direction of causation may be ambiguous (e.g., Do high expectations cause high achievement or the reverse?); and the ever-present failing—"More research is needed."

Read this book constructively and creatively. Think about what the information and strategies mean for school organization, staff and student attitudes, and teaching and learning, that is, for your own professional success and satisfaction and for the learning and success of your students.

We are indebted to Kay Van Der Burg, Palo Alto, California, Public Schools, and Bonnie L. Williams, University of Wisconsin—Madison, whose work contributed to several sections of this book. We would also like to acknowledge those individuals who reviewed this book at various stages: Sandra Baker, Munster, Indiana, Public Schools, and Lewis Romano, Michigan State University.

G. A. D.
M. A. T.

Chapter One

Thinking about Effective Schools

*We can, whenever and wherever we choose, successfully
teach all children whose schooling is of interest to us;
we already know more than we need to do that.*
—Ronald R. Edmonds, "Effective Schools for the Urban Poor"

*This is an exciting time to be part of the educational
community.*
—William E. Bickel, "Effective Schools: Knowledge, Dissemination,
Inquiry"

A remarkable revolution is in progress in our thinking about good
schools and good teaching: Educators are showing an increasingly
keen interest in the objective, scientific analysis of attitudes and
practices that affect student achievement. While research on
teaching has existed for many decades, the past 15 years have
seen monumental advances in our understanding of the extent of
the effects that the goals and leadership behavior of principals, the
management and instructional practices of teachers, and the culture and climate of schools and classrooms have on student
achievement.

Many findings and recommendations amount to common
sense—teaching habits instinctively adopted by every effective
teacher. Foremost among these is the pedagogical principle that
the more students study the more they learn. This disarmingly obvious universal truth follows on the heels of 50 years of searching
for teacher characteristics and behavior patterns that are causally
related to student achievement. It has earned the titles *academic
engagement, academic engaged time* (Rosenshine & Berliner,

1978), *academic learning time* (Denham & Lieberman, 1980), time spent in *direct instruction* (Rosenshine, 1979), and *time on task*. It has inspired superintendents, principals, and teachers to ensure that adequate time is allocated to the basics, time-use guidelines are followed, time blocks are protected from interruption, time spent on noninstructional activities is minimized, incomplete tasks are finished, and extra learning time is provided to students who need it. A common educational change in the 1980s has been to lengthen the school day and the school year, as has been done in the state of California (Odden, 1988).

Bickel (1983) put it this way: "As often happens when old truths are discovered, the notion that instructional time is crucial for learning, particularly among children and youth who have not yet become independent learners, has been the biggest news in education for the past few years."

Another great truth in the common-sense category is the revelation that scores on students' achievement tests will be higher if they are directed to study the material to be covered on the test (Berliner, 1984; Squires, Huitt, & Segars, 1983). This principle is called *criterion-related instruction, appropriate coverage,* or just *overlap,* referring to the degree of overlap of the content of instruction with the content of the test. The significance—and there is great significance—is that if teachers and administrators are serious about raising scores on achievement tests, they should attend closely to the degree of overlap. Researchers have discovered that overlap can range from a miniscule 4% to 95% (Brady, Clinton, Sweeney, Peterson, & Poyner, 1977). Many principals and teachers concerned with improving school effectiveness do, in fact, focus their instructional efforts on the content of the achievement tests.

Before concluding that time spent reading this book could more profitably be used in other ways, be assured that

1. Research has uncovered many fine-grained, specific, and unexpected attitudes and behaviors of teachers and principals that relate to student achievement.

2. Educational reforms based in part on this research have led to improvements in student achievement, self-concepts, and school attitudes; improvements in teachers' instructional skills and sense of professional efficacy; principals' expertise in managing reforms; improved teaching of at-risk and special needs children; and a clearer vision of school goals for administrators, staff, and students (T. Peterson, 1988).

3. Teachers who attend closely to the research findings and recommendations in these pages and constructively relate them to their own teaching will be better teachers—effective in promoting higher achievement and better academic attitudes, self-reflective and analytic in evaluating their own teaching, and respected and liked by students and colleagues.

The remainder of this chapter summarizes background information and some preliminary issues and dilemmas to help readers interpret the research and take a more sophisticated perspective on it.

THE COLEMAN REPORT

The most frequently cited conclusion of the well-known Coleman Report (Coleman et al., 1966) is that differences among schools in the amount of money they spend on education and even on teaching itself had little impact on ultimate student achievement. What did seem to make a difference was family background, social class, northern versus southern school location, urban versus rural school setting, and peer influence and traditions. In short, nonschool factors appeared to be more important than school variables. The widely read *Inequality: A Reassessment of Family and Schooling in America* by Christopher Jencks and his colleagues (1972; see also Miller, 1983) reached basically the same conclusions. One extreme position even argued that because the educational system adequately educated only the middle and upper classes, the system was a tool for perpetuating an unequal class structure (Bowles & McGintis, 1976). In 1974 Averch, Carroll, Donaldson, Kiesling, and Pincus published a comprehensive and authoritative review of planned efforts to raise achievement levels. It pessimistically concluded that no particular intervention strategy for improving education was sufficiently effective to guide national policy.

Because of the high visibility and impact of the Coleman Report and related literature, which concluded that schools (and by implication principals and teachers) made little or no difference, several of the cornerstone research projects in the effective-schooling movement were compelled to prove first that effective schools did in fact exist (e.g., Edmonds, 1979; Rutter, Maugham, Mortimore, Ouston, & Smith, 1979; Weber, 1971). They asked, given student body compositions of equal socioeconomic level, were some schools better able to teach basic skills than others? The answer, of course, was a resounding yes; effective schools did indeed exist. Their intuitions confirmed, the researchers proceeded with the next logical step—searching for characteristics that seemed to be related to that effectiveness.

Before leaving the Coleman Report, we should make two additional comments. First, the Coleman Report and related documents that seemed to support it were both right and wrong. On one hand, there is no question that family and community factors, particularly socioeconomic status (SES), do indeed affect school achievement. Nonetheless, as you will discover throughout this book, there is overwhelming evidence that school structure, school climate, leadership, and teaching practices make a profound difference in student achievement and attitudes toward school. Moreover, to improve their own effectiveness, administrators and teachers can adopt most of these patterns and strategies to raise achievement levels (e.g., Good & Grouws, 1979). In fact, most states and many individual school districts have created school improvement programs based on the main findings of the effective-schooling literature (e.g., Austin, 1979; Bickel, 1983; Brookover, 1981; Buttram & Kruse, 1988; Clark & McCarthy, 1983; Edmonds, 1978, 1979, 1981, 1982; Mackenzie, 1983; McCormack-Larkin & Kritek, 1983; Odden, 1988; Peterson, 1988; Willms & Raudenbush, 1988). The deep pessimism and fatalism of the 1960s was misdirected.

Our second comment on the Coleman Report and related documents is that their depressing conclusions led to a psychological climate among educators and researchers in the 1970s that was ready for a more optimistic message. The logical and sensible results of the early effective-schooling studies confirmed that administrators, principals, and teachers could indeed take positive steps to improve education; things were not as bad as Coleman had led them to believe. Furthermore, every educator personally knew of successful schools and good teachers, and the findings of the effective-schooling literature squared well with their strong intuitive beliefs (Bickel, 1983).

TEACHING AS AN ART AND A SCIENCE

Effective-schooling leader Nathaniel Gage (1978, 1984, 1985) has explained many times that teaching is both an art and a science. According to him, it is an "instrumental, practical art" rather than a "fine art." That is, teaching "requires improvisation, spontaneity, the handling of a vast array of considerations of form, style, pace, rhythm, and appropriateness in ways so complex that even computers must lose the way" (1984). In short, the teaching process is too complex, with a nearly infinite variety of circumstances, subjects, student groups, and age groups, to be reduced to simple how-to-do-it recipes.

At the same time, according to Gage, teaching can and should have a scientific basis. Science deals with relationships between both input (independent) variables and output (dependent) variables. A sizable amount of good research has been carried out that relates teaching and administrative practices to student achievement as well as motivation, attitudes, and self-esteem (Gage, 1984).

INSTRUCTION AND MANAGEMENT

For decades, research on teaching and guides for classroom management followed independent pathways. In retrospect this independence seems astonishing because the two are in fact inseparable. In Chapter 4 we will see that such well-confirmed management principles as "withitness" (letting students know that you know what is going on), using variety to reduce boredom, and making smooth transitions between activities simultaneously reduce disruptions and increase student engagement and learning. Good management is essential for effective teaching.

CRITERIA OF EFFECTIVENESS

Throughout the research on effective schools and effective teaching, the main criterion of effectiveness has been higher achievement, virtually always measured by standardized tests of reading and/or mathematics. The reasons for this seemingly narrow definition of *effectiveness* are straightforward: Reading and mathematics achievement are obviously important goals of education that almost no one will question. Standardized test scores are impressive and acceptable to school administrators, teachers, parents, and the public alike. Furthermore, widely accepted standardized tests do not exist for many other desirable educational outcomes.

However, there *are* other legitimate goals of a truly effective school. Most of these goals require class time that, logically, is at the expense of time spent on the basics. For example, another revolution in education is a growing interest in teaching thinking skills such as creativity; problem solving; critical thinking; metaphorical thinking; Bloom's (1974) application, analysis, synthesis, and evaluation skills; and many more (see Davis & Rimm, 1989, for an overview). Many schools also must try to teach good self-concepts, good citizenship, independence, academic motivation, interpersonal skills, and values and moral thinking. These student-centered goals aim at helping students, especially those in at-risk groups, think better of themselves, gain control over their destinies, and reduce antisocial and self-destructive behaviors such as drug and alcohol abuse, dropping out, and crime. Other legitimate goals of effective schools can include designing optimal educational conditions for special populations such as retarded, slow learning, emotionally disturbed, learning disabled, handicapped, and gifted students.

There are important subject areas other than math and reading, and there are other values, skills, and knowledge that society agrees are valuable, but whose teaching may not contribute to improvements in those highly visible reading and math scores. Of course, the principles derived from effective schooling research that pertain to raising math and reading achievement are appropriate for improving the teaching of most other subjects.

While researchers and administrators in the 1970s and into the 1980s emphasized, or even overemphasized, improved mathematics and reading scores as measures of effectiveness, the National School Recognition Program listed the following as indicators of effective schools (Sergiovanni, 1987):

1. Improved test scores.

2. Improved attendance.

3. A generally increased number of writing and homework assignments, with the amount of homework based on the age of the students.

4. Increased instructional time spent on mathematics, English, science, history and social science, foreign languages, and fine arts.

5. Community and parent participation.

6. Student participation in extracurricular activities.

7. Awards and recognition for students and teachers.

8. Quality of support for students with special needs.

In Chapter 6 we will describe *second-wave reform* (Lieberman, 1988; Michaels, 1988), which has emerged in the late 1980s. While first-wave reform stressed raising standards in mathematics, science, and English; using more intelligent textbooks; holding teachers and students accountable; lengthening the school day and year; increasing high school graduation requirements; and generally increasing the rigor of American education; second-wave reform includes, for example, teaching thinking skills, teaching students to understand "why," and fostering a more collegial environment among both students and staff.

OBSERVATIONAL, CORRELATIONAL, AND EXPERIMENTAL RESEARCH

As a general trend, research on effective schooling has progressed through the following three phases:

1. *Observational* and *case study* research identifies factors of school climate and apparently successful teaching and management methods.

2. *Correlational* studies show statistical relationships among variables but do not absolutely confirm causality. For example, high achievement may cause high teacher and principal expectations rather than the reverse (Rowan, Bossert, & Dwyer, 1983); or both high expectations and high achievement may be caused by a third factor such as high student intelligence (Good & Brophy, 1985).

3. *Experimental* studies using experimental (trained) teachers and control teachers concretely demonstrate that certain teaching or management practices adopted by teachers in regular classrooms will indeed cause higher student achievement.

While observational, correlational, and experimental research have evolved in that order, all three types continue to be conducted. However, of the three, there have been comparatively few experimental studies.

TEACHING TO THE TESTS
AND INFLATING TEST SCORES

There is no doubt that increasing the degree of overlap of instruction with the content of achievement tests (*criterion-related instruction*) will raise achievement scores and make teachers, principal, and school look more effective.

Is so-called teaching to the test a trivial accomplishment or an important and profound one? Probably both. Higher achievement scores mean something in these days of accountability. If reading and mathematics scores are low, a school and its staff will not be judged successful or effective by the public, school board, parents, or even its students. Two-page spreads appear in major newspapers listing the math and reading scores for hundreds of elementary schools in dozens of districts. No superintendent, school board, principal, or teacher wants to be made to look bad in public.

Webster (1988) described how, according to one survey, only 12% of the teachers felt that achievement scores were the most important outcome of schooling. These teachers rated improved self-concepts, better school attitudes, and an improved school climate as more important. However, a full 98% of parents and school board members rated achievement scores as the most important outcome. According to Webster, the parents and school board members conceded that the other outcomes are fine as long as achievement scores are high.

Actually, teaching to the tests may not be simple. A local district curriculum guide defines the content to be taught, and this may or may not match the content of an achievement test published in San Francisco, Iowa City, or Princeton, New Jersey. Teachers have their own opinions about which topics are important, and so do principals, parents, and school boards. Beyond this, different published tests emphasize different content. For example, a survey of fourth-grade mathematics tests by Floden, Porter, Schmidt, and Freeman (1980) showed that the proportion of test items using whole numbers varied from 39% in one test to 66% in another.

To complicate matters even more, school textbooks traditionally have been written without awareness of achievement test content. The authors of the texts probably have not been worried about overlap; besides, they would not know which standardized test to use as a guide. Comparing the content of standardized tests with the content of mathematics textbooks, Floden and colleagues found that in the worst case 47% of the fourth-grade topics tested were not covered by the text; the best case showed only 71% overlap.

One solution suggested by Squires, Huitt, and Segars (1983), who accept criterion-related instruction (overlap) as a good road to increased achievement, is for the school or district to develop curriculum guides that include the majority of the content to be tested. Another suggested solution was to find and adopt a textbook that overlaps substantially with the achievement test used. Perhaps the best solution is for the individual district to develop its own achievement tests—tests that will reflect the content of printed district goals and guides.

Confidentially, principals and teachers do more than just teach to the tests in order to raise scores in reading and mathematics. To make themselves and their schools appear more effective, some principals deliberately exclude certain groups from achievement testing, for example, learning disabled, handicapped, and educable mentally retarded students. Some principals also announce in advance when the tests will be given, with a tacit understanding that students who are anxious about the testing can miss school that day with no questions asked. One unnamed state in which the average Scholastic Aptitude Test (SAT) scores were at the top nationally was simultaneously at the bottom in the proportion of students who actually took the test. Teachers have been known to wander the aisles during testing, giving students clear cues when they spot mistakes, perhaps clearing their throats, making clucking sounds, or just pausing and staring.

There are both pragmatic problems and conflicts of conscience with the issue of teaching to the tests, to say nothing of the questionable actions taken to artificially inflate average class, grade, or school achievement scores. In practice, according to Haggerson (1988), most teachers take a middle-of-the-road approach, teaching to the tests to ensure decent test scores, but covering other academic, affective, and process topics as well.

INTERRELATIONSHIPS AMONG FACTORS

In later chapters many important variables influencing student behavior and achievement will be discussed. It is important to realize that many environmental, teaching, and management factors are interrelated; thus a weakness in one may be tied to deficiencies in others. For example, Squires, Huitt, and Segars (1983) identified student involvement (academic engagement), amount of content covered, and student success levels in daily work and unit tests as the three most important indicators of an effective classroom. They noted that if academic engagement is low it may be due to an inadequate time allocation, unnecessary disruptions requiring better management procedures, or the way in which students are socialized to the achievement norms of the school and classroom. Similarly, if success levels are low educators should examine the scope and sequence of learning tasks, methods of instruction, feedback provided to students, and how all of these relate to student characteristics.

In the middle school or high school, low success levels may be due to variations in students' preparation. Pretesting is required to determine each student's current level of knowledge and skill.

SOCIOECONOMIC LEVEL

Please make no mistake about our view: Achievement levels can be improved in all schools and with all student groups. However, in lower socioeconomic (SES) areas you also get lower academic motivation, lower long-term educational and career aspirations, less family and community support for school achievement, peer values of rebelliousness and disdain for schools and teachers, and therefore lower average achievement. According to Walberg's (1985) synthesis of research on teaching, 97.6% of 620 studies showed a relationship of social class to learning and achievement. Stimulating high achievement in lower SES schools will be challenging, to say the least.

CURVILINEAR RELATIONSHIPS OF
TEACHING PRACTICES WITH ACHIEVEMENT

The interpretation of results of research on effective schools and teachers may not be a simple and linear "the more of this you do, the more of that you get." There may be an intermediate level that produces the highest achievement or the best attitudes; that is, the relationship may be curvilinear. For example, in one study of the effects of success rates in second-grade reading, achievement scores peaked when students' success rate was about 75% (Squires, Huitt, & Segars, 1983). Achievement decreased with higher levels of success. The tasks became too easy; they were no longer interesting and challenging. Crawford, King, Brophy, and Evertson (1975) similarly found that the optimal level of correct answers to teachers' oral questions was around 75%. Homework and high teacher expectations both have been found to relate to student achievement. However, a teacher can assign too little or too much homework or have expectations that are too low or too high.

According to Brophy and Good (1985), *all* classroom variables are curvilinear in their effects on achievement—there can be too much or too little of any teaching or management practice. To complicate matters further, the optimal level of a given teaching practice can vary depending on the particular subject, the grade, the students, or other factors.

CENTRAL TENDENCIES PLUS VARIABILITY

Correlational and experimental research always deals with *central tendencies* plus *variability*. In effective-schooling research, teaching practice *A* will be related to a higher average achievement measure *B*. However, there also will be variability around this average achievement score. Some of this variability will be due to random error of measurement. On the other hand, with some grade levels, subjects, classrooms, or student groups the effects of a particular teaching practice will be systematically greater or less than the average effect reported in the research. It is the broad trends—the central tendencies—that should guide teaching and management practices. As Gage (1985) put it, "The wise researcher, teacher educator, or teacher will use the central tendencies for all they are worth. . . . But the same wise person will also be sensitive to the uniqueness of every classroom and student and alert to the likelihood of departures from the central tendencies."

That is, there may be *patterns* in the variation as well as in the central tendencies, and perceptive teachers should attend to both. For example, in a school-wide improvement program there may be unique and informative patterns among some student age groups, SES groups, or ethnic groups in their responses to changes in school climate or teaching practices.

SCHOOL EFFECTS? PRINCIPAL EFFECTS? TEACHER EFFECTS?

As we will see in Chapter 3, research on effective schools tends to focus on school-level characteristics. The main characteristics of effective schools that have emerged from the research, and which have become classic, include the following:

1. Strong instructional leadership.

2. High expectations for student achievement.

3. A safe and orderly learning environment.

4. An emphasis on basic skills.

5. Continuous monitoring of student progress.

6. Clear and well-understood school goals.

While item 1 recognizes the importance of the principal, many educators strongly emphasize that it is *only* the energetic and dedicated principal who is in the unique position to lead the school staff and students toward school goals. According to Ubben and Hughes (1987), "One is struck with the absolute necessity of creative leadership by the principal for an effective learning climate to occur. . . . Effective schools are the result of the activities of effective principals." Mackenzie (1983) similarly noted that the discovery of the crucial role of the principal as an instructional leader "played a catalytic role in what is felt to be the breakthrough in effective schools research." Chapter 2 will further elucidate the monumental influence of an effective principal in increasing school success.

At the same time, of course, it is neither principals nor schools who face and teach students every day; it is teachers. Individual teachers may or may not be successful in leading students to higher levels of learning and higher aspirations in ways that are interesting and motivating.

Rowan, Bossert, and Dwyer (1983) said of this issue that research has not clarified exactly "how school-level factors [items 1–6 above] affect the process of teaching and learning that ultimately leads to increased achievement by students."

As you read the following chapters on effective principals, effective schools, and effective teachers, you may wish to consider the contributions that stem from each perspective as well as interrelationships among the perspectives that combine into ideas for effective schooling and higher student achievement. Consider also the implications for other important outcomes such as good self-concepts and school attitudes, improved thinking skills, and better teaching of at-risk students and those with special needs.

IS THE EFFECTIVE–SCHOOLS MOVEMENT A PASSING FAD?

Some scholars do see the effective-schooling movement as something of a new fad—the teaching machines and new math of the 1980s. Sirotnik (1985), for example, called the movement "a bandwagon in search of a tune." Rowan (1984) claimed that there is a "cultlike belief in the mystical and curative powers" of the major recommendations emanating from effective-schooling research.

It is clear to us, however, that the principles of effective schooling are logical and sound, they do in fact improve instruction, and they can be adopted successfully. Now, more than ever before, there is a knowledge base for dealing with problems. The overriding challenge is to help more administrators and teachers design and implement programs and teaching practices that take advantage of proven correlates of higher achievement.

There is little doubt that a knowledge of research on effective schools and effective teachers can raise awareness of some of what schools and teachers are doing right and what they are doing wrong. Those who are or will be teachers can be guided by this knowledge to improve their own teaching and classroom management habits.

SUMMARY

Research on effective schooling is fascinating in its focus on school, principal, and teacher factors that are consistently associated with higher student achievement. The findings challenge dedicated administrators and teachers to reexamine their existing philosophies and practices and modify them in accordance with research-based, intuitively sound guidelines. Many states and districts are doing so.

Many core recommendations derive from common sense, for example, the principle of academic engagement and the notion that test scores can be raised by increasing the overlap of teaching with testing.

The effective schooling movement was inspired partly by the claim of the Coleman Report that social and economic factors far outweigh any effects of schools and teachers; that is, "schools make no difference." The effective-schooling answer is that while socioeconomic status (SES) does influence school attitudes and achievement, school academic climate, leadership, and teaching and management practices can be engineered to improve student achievement and other important educational outcomes regardless of SES or other demographic characteristics.

Gage emphasized that, due to its complexity, teaching is a form of "practical art." At the same time, teaching also should be guided by scientific research; it is an art *and* a science.

Despite their previous independent treatment in the research literature, classroom management and teaching practices are actually interwoven.

Research on effective schooling emphasizes (or overemphasizes) achievement in reading and mathematics as the criterion for school and teaching effectiveness, due to the obvious importance and the ready measurement of these subjects. However, there are other important educational subjects and more student-centered outcomes, for example, development of thinking skills, good self-concepts and other affective goals, and accommodation of the needs of special groups. Second-wave reform of the late 1980s recognizes a broader spectrum of valuable outcomes, for example, teaching for understanding and creating a more collegial student—teacher environment.

Research has progressed from observational and case study approaches through correlational studies to experimental research that confirms cause—effect relationships. All three remain popular, although experimental research is rare.

So-called teaching to the tests, or criterion-related instruction, may require compromise in goals and plans. To complicate matters, standardized tests differ in their coverage of various topics, and different textbooks overlap to different degrees with published tests.

Administrators sometimes inflate reading and mathematics scores by exempting certain student groups from testing or by allowing worried students to miss the tests. Teachers may subtly signal students when errors are made.

Many environmental, teaching, and management factors are so interrelated that weaknesses in one may be caused by problems in another. For example, low academic engagement may be caused by a nonacademic climate or poor classroom management procedures. SES level is related to academic motivation, educational and career aspirations, family and community support, peer influences, and, therefore, achievement.

Many, perhaps all, variables identified in research on effective schooling have a curvilinear relationship with achievement such that an intermediate level (e.g., of homework or expectations) is optimal.

Educators should attend to central tendencies, the average achievement levels attained by altering teaching or management practices. They also must be sensitive to systematic variability, due perhaps to the uniqueness of a classroom or to the reactions of certain age or ethnic groups to a given innovation.

Effective-schools research focuses on school-level characteristics that relate to higher achievement. At the same time, informed educators recognize that instructional leadership by an energetic principal is crucial for school success. Further, it is teachers who actually teach students and manage classrooms. Readers should remain sensitive to the contributions and interrelationships of school, principal, and teacher factors that promote good school attitudes and higher achievement.

While some consider the effective-schooling movement to be a passing fad, most are convinced that the principles are too sound to be ignored. The principles raise awareness of effective and ineffective schooling practices and serve as guides to improve teaching and management skills and increase feelings of professional efficacy.

Chapter Two

Effective Principals

I have never seen a good school with a poor principal or a poor school with a good principal. I have seen unsuccessful schools turned around into successful ones and, regrettably, outstanding schools slide rapidly into decline. In each case the rise or fall could readily be traced to the quality of the principal.
—Fred M. Hechinger, Foreword to James M. Lipham, *Effective Principal, Effective School*

In schools that were extremely good we inevitably found an aggressive, professionally alert, dynamic principal determined to provide the kind of educational program he/she deemed necessary, no matter what.
—Keith Goldhammer and Gerald L. Becker, *Elementary School Principals and Their Schools*

It is the leadership of the school that makes the difference between mediocrity and excellence.
—Gerald L. Ubben and Lawrence W. Hughes, *The Principal: Creative Leadership for Effective Schools*

It is ironic that in the early years of searching for characteristics of effective teaching, researchers look right past the single most important factor in overall school success—the vision, dedication, energy, and instructional leadership of the principal. Fortunately, in recent years, strong instructional leadership has appeared on virtually every thoughtful list of characteristics of effective schooling (e.g., Achilles, 1987; Blumberg & Greenfield, 1980; Brookover et al., 1979; Edmonds, 1979; Good & Brophy, 1985; Lipham, 1981; Phi Delta Kappa, 1980; Purkey & Smith, 1983; Rutherford, 1985; Ubben & Hughes, 1987; Wynne, 1981).

A capsule description of the qualities and behaviors that characterize principals in successful schools—qualities that have surfaced again and again in the research literature—runs as follows:

- Effective principals have a strong vision of what their schools can be, and they encourage all staff to work toward realizing that vision.
- They hold high expectations for both student achievement and staff performance.
- They observe teachers in classrooms and provide positive, constructive feedback aimed at solving problems and improving instruction.
- They encourage efficient use of instructional time and design procedures to minimize disruptions.
- They use material and personnel resources creatively.
- They monitor the individual and collective achievement of students and use the information to guide instructional planning.

Unfortunately, many less effective principals define their role as manager of the building and budget, keeper of the records, chief disciplinarian, and communicator with everyone. They leave the teaching to teachers. Research on the activities and behavior of principals indicates that most principals spend very little time on curriculum and instructional matters (Martin & Willower, 1981; Willower & Kmetz, 1982). The truth is that few principals have been prepared for instructional leadership (Goodlad, 1983).

Most teachers, parents, and interested others are unaware of the pivotal role an instructionally active principal can play in creating an effective school—a school where everyone is concerned with learning and achievement, expectations are high, and educational improvement is a daily concern.

THE WORK OF THE PRINCIPAL

The daily routine of every principal—although *routine* is hardly the correct word—includes activities described as "varied and disjointed" by Lee (1987) and "varied, brief and fragmented" by Martin and Willower (1981). Greenfield (1987) concluded that the activities of principals involve "an endless series of brief interpersonal encounters and exchanges with students, teachers, parents, superiors, and others." According to Blumberg (1987), "What we find . . . is an image of people who spend their days in a highly fragmented manner, moving from one problematic situation to another, having a minimum of time to devote to these situations and even less time to reflect on them." Many tasks are left unfinished while others demand attention. The work is a stream of unanticipated questions, problems, and situations, most of which have little to do with teaching and learning.

Most principals begin their daily activities by confirming that classrooms are staffed and that substitute teachers are managing their classes well. Throughout the day they monitor work operations; schedule, organize, and allocate resources; and deal with matters of safety and orderliness.

The work is largely verbal. They dispense information about procedures and policies to veteran teachers, new teachers, substitute teachers, special education teachers, reading specialists, counselors, school psychologists, maintenance staff, students, parents, and others in the community. They answer questions about the availability of aides, space, materials and other resources, and details about forthcoming events. They act as intermediaries between the district office and the school staff. They help organize field trips, intermural sports, and academic teams. They work with multidisciplinary (M) teams on behalf of individual students. They talk with police and probation officers and fire department officials, for whom they schedule up to eight fire drills per year. Other than the school nurse, a principal may be the only person permitted by insurance companies to dispense medication to students.

Principals must deal with competing values and expectations along with shortages in space, staff, funds, equipment, and materials. Misunderstandings, conflicts, and miscommunications are common (Dwyer, 1984; Dwyer, Lee, Barnett, Filby, & Rowan, 1984).

In an effort to make sense of the typical principal's activities, Morris, Crowson, Hurwitz, and Porter-Gehrie (1982) classified the principal's work day into monitoring school activities, serving as school spokesperson, disseminating information to school staff, handling disturbances, and allocating resources. They concluded that "everything seems to blend together in an undifferentiated jumble of activities . . . [related] . . . to the ongoing rhythm and purpose of the larger enterprise."

Blumberg (1987) asked elementary school principals to describe their job activities metaphorically. A lighthearted list of 63 metaphors included firefighter, detective, superteacher, toll taker, quarterback, Red Cross worker, psychiatrist, distance runner, coach, judge, choreographer, paper chaser, hospital orderly, prostitute, and professor. Based on considerable experience with the work of principals, Blumberg decided that such metaphors do indeed describe the meaning of leadership in the elementary school, at least in part.

Taking into account mundane activities such as being visible after school so that buses are boarded efficiently, heavy-duty responsibilities such as dealing with an incompetent teacher, and the 63 metaphors, Blumberg summarized the principal's work as activities aimed at

- Keeping things going as peacefully as possible.
- Dealing with conflict or avoiding it.
- Healing wounds.
- Supervising the work of others.
- Developing the organization.
- Implementing educational ideas.

Blumberg concluded that the work of a school principal resembles a highly skilled craft, rather than an art or an applied science.

In their studies of effective principals, Dwyer, Lee, Rowan, and Bossert (1983) and Dwyer and colleagues (1984) reported that in all instances principals held a working theory that guided their actions. That working theory was based upon their experience, the characteristics of the community and district, and the instructional climate and organization of the school.

Dwyer, Lee, Rowan, and Bossert (1982) were particularly impressed with the high energy and activity levels of their effective principals. These principals roam the building as children arrive, making certain that classrooms are staffed and ready, then return to their offices for planning, telephoning, and the first round of daily student problems. At recess time they are in the halls again—monitoring, communicating with staff, and solving problems. Between recess and lunch they move in and out of classes, observing and talking with teachers and students. Early afternoon is consumed with discipline problems requiring interaction with students, teachers, and parents. The final bell brings the principals back to the hallways "where they admonish or praise, prompt or prohibit in rapid-fire encounters." The final, calm minutes of the day are spent in reflection, parent conferences, teacher conferences, or staff or committee meetings.

Overall, it is not surprising that only part of the workday of effective principals—and little or no time of other principals—is spent directly supervising and improving instruction.

DEFINITION OF INSTRUCTIONAL LEADERSHIP

Because instructional leadership is the subject of this chapter, and indeed much of the entire book, we should look briefly at what it is. Instructional improvement and educational reform are at its center. According to DeBevoise (1984), instructional leadership means "those actions that a principal takes, or delegates to others, to promote growth in student learning." Effective-schooling leader Greenfield (1987) has defined *instructional leadership* as "actions undertaken with the intention of developing a productive and satisfying working environment for teachers and desirable learning conditions and outcomes for children," adding that "such leadership is effective to the extent that these broad purposes are achieved."

The following three core ideas related to the instructional leadership role of the principal are closely tied to the characteristics and behaviors of effective principals described in the following sections:

- Effective principals hold an image or vision of what they want to accomplish.

- This vision guides principals in managing and leading their schools.

- Effective principals focus their activities on instruction and the classroom performance of teachers (Greenfield, 1987; Manasse, 1985).

INSTRUCTIONAL LEADERSHIP AND EMPOWERING TEACHERS: A CONFLICT?

The effective schooling literature has firmly established that strong leadership by the principal is essential to a successful and innovative school, and this emphasis continues unabated. However, a current healthy trend, part of second-wave reform (Chapter 6), is toward giving teachers more authority. *Empower* is the buzzword. More and more teachers are empowered to make decisions regarding curriculum and instruction, planning and implementing programs, and other matters (Buttram & Kruse, 1988; McClure, 1988). The role of teachers is changing; they are viewed as experts and the principal as a manager of experts.

On the surface, it appears that there could be a conflict between fulfilling the traditional leadership role of the principal and delegating part of that authority to teachers. However, there should be little or no conflict in settings where principals and teachers work together for school improvement. Leadership is shared according to who has the competency for a particular job (McClure, 1988). The principal sets the stage and empowers dedicated teachers to implement the agenda. The principal creates the climate, sets the school-wide goals, provides inservice training in effective teaching skills, helps plan and implement new programs, and monitors the results in order to reach goals of continued growth.

VISION, SCHOOL CLIMATE, AND EXPECTATIONS

Vision

Descriptions of principals of effective schools emphasize their *vision*—their image of what the school can be and what they want to accomplish. Colton (1985) defined vision as that "which establishes goals or objectives for individual and group action, which defines not what we are but rather what we seek to be or do." According to Greenfield (1987), vision or "moral imagination" is

> *the inclination of a person to see that . . . the school and associated activities of teaching and learning need not remain as it is—that it is possible for it to be otherwise, and to be better. . . . It is the ability to see the discrepancy between how things are and how they might be—not in terms of the ideal, but in terms of what is possible, given a particular school situation.*

Vision is a critical antecedent to effective leadership. Through daily interactions and modeling, the principal transmits his or her vision of a better school to teachers and other staff and influences them to act to achieve that vision. Rutherford (1985) noted that when a principal has a strong vision for the future of a school, most teachers become aware of and accept that vision. Of course, the principal's vision is influenced by school board policy, the superintendent's philosophy, and community norms and expectations.

Dwyer and his colleagues (1982) also have stressed that effective principals have coherent visions of what their school should be and attempt to realize these visions in their daily work. Their vision guides such high-energy activities as continually assessing how well the school is functioning, suggesting improvements in teaching styles, and reacting to student misbehavior in a fair and appropriate manner. Their vision-guided daily activities do indeed have a profound impact on the quality of instruction and student achievement (Dwyer et al., 1982).

Rutherford (1985) asked principals of both effective and ineffective schools, "What is your vision for this school—your long-range goals and expectations?" With no hesitation, effective principals responded in an enthusiastic way that reflected their belief in such goals as finding ways to meet the learning needs of all students, helping teachers adjust to a changing school population, raising test scores in a specific content area, or "turning out more National Merit Scholars." As Rutherford noted, "They led the band and made things happen."

Less effective principals usually answered, after a lengthy pause, with something like the following:

> "We have a good school and a good faculty and I want us to keep it that way."

> "I have heard some of the recommendations from the commission reports, and I think that we are already doing most of those things."

> "We want to have a safe and orderly school."

Alternatively, they referred to written goals and requirements prepared by the school district, state education agency, or an accrediting association. Rutherford concluded that "the less effective principals had no vision for their schools; they focused on maintaining tranquility in the here and now."

How is vision developed? Many energetic, effective principals just seem to have it. Others, according to Achilles (1987), are able to develop and become committed to a vision of a better school by (a) reading the literature on effective schools—which inevitably stresses the principal's vision—and (b) visiting effective schools and learning what can happen with effective leadership.

Academic School Climate and High Expectations

The principal's vision is logically and intimately tied to two other premier and frequently cited characteristics of effective schools— an academic school climate (or culture) and high expectations for student achievement.

Generally, an organizational climate or culture consists of shared values, rules, ideology, goals, and conceptions regarding the organization. Walter and Stanfield (1988) said of the importance of school culture that "culture is the 'normative glue,' the consistency in values that holds the organization together."

In an academic climate, staff and students are aware of and they value goals of high achievement. Researchers agree that principals, influenced by school boards and district superintendents, play a vital role in creating such an atmosphere through their beliefs, attitudes, expectations, and activities. Cohen (1983), for example, reported that effective principals emphasize high achievement and express optimism about the ability of all students to meet instructional goals. Blum (1984) similarly found that effective principals believe and emphasize to staff that learning is the most important reason for students to be in school; that all children can learn; and that school makes the difference between success and failure. Good and Brophy (1985) also stressed that effective principals are able to create a strong sense of community that includes shared values and culture, common goals, and high expectations for both student achievement and the staff performance that creates it.

Said one teacher in a school with a strong academic orientation, "I have taught in other states and other schools, but until I came here I never realized how enjoyable teaching could be. It is not that the students are better; it is just that everyone here seems to value learning." And another teacher commented, "We're all pulling together" (Rutherford, 1985).

In less effective schools, teachers tend not to share a common understanding of school-wide goals and expectations. If goals are mentioned at all, it usually is in regard to personal goals or else department goals in secondary schools.

There is also an affective side to a favorable school climate or culture. Cohen (1983), for example, pointed out that a good sense of school community requires not only shared goals but the creation of a moral order that includes respect for authority, mutual trust, and a genuine caring about individuals and their feelings and attitudes. Odden (1988) similarly mentioned staff collegiality, staff–student collegiality, and, again, "caring attitudes about kids" as important parts of the school climate.

In Chapter 6 we shall see how educators are looking to successful corporations to learn about strategies for creating strong organizational cultures that lead to higher productivity and company spirit. For example, companies such as Apple Computer, IBM, and Walt Disney Productions shape values by making heroes of those who exemplify company values and by establishing rituals, ceremonies, and company slogans that illustrate what the company stands for.

CREATING AN ACADEMIC CLIMATE

Principals can take many concrete steps to aid the development of an academic orientation and high achievement expectations, virtually all of which reflect their instructional leadership role. The following eight categories of suggestions stem from research on the observations of effective schools and effective principals.

1. Principals can take an active and personal role in raising awareness of the need for school improvement and higher achievement expectations and gaining consensus for the changes. For example, they can communicate the expectation that instructional programs can and will improve over time. Especially, principals can empower teachers to work together to plan and incorporate improvements. They can ensure that instructional improvement strategies are given high priority and high visibility. Principals also can create procedures for eliciting parent and community support for improvement plans, for example, by speaking at PTA meetings.

Principals can help build consensus on school rules and patterns of acceptable behavior among staff, students, and administration that are consistent with and promote an academic orientation.

2. Principals can be active in creating the concrete improvements themselves. For example, they can plan, secure, and monitor inservice staff development opportunities, obtaining staff input on the content of the training; be active and supportive in helping teachers learn to use new instructional approaches; and establish expectations for good curriculum quality through the use of standards and guidelines. They can help staff establish priorities and plan instructional improvements; supervise and coordinate implementation of plan components; and monitor the results.

Principals also can actively elicit parent involvement in the school's instructional efforts, for example, by enlisting parent time as office and classroom aides, parent energy in organizing school-wide festivities, and parent money for expansion of school programs (Hallinger & Murphy, 1987).

3. Principals can create reward systems for students and teachers that support an academic orientation and stimulate excellence in student and teacher performance. For example, they can help create motivational devices such as school slogans, buttons, T-shirts, or songs emphasizing school identity and academic achievement. Walter and Stanfield (1988) described how school slogans help create proper values for teachers and students: "A fair break for every child"; "A child's right to an education is non-negotiable"; "Move out of the comfort zone"; and "Win with class; lose with dignity."

One popular strategy is the use of posters that proclaim to anyone entering the building (i.e., students, teachers, parents, community members, and others) the vision, expectations, mission, direction, and goals of a school.

Principals can make certain that student, staff, and school accomplishments and awards are visible in the building and to parents and the public. Good public relations work through newspapers, radio, and television can strengthen school pride and school identity.

By praising good work and individual strengths, and by taking an interest in their personal well-being, principals can develop and maintain positive staff relations.

4. A central and well-documented behavior of effective principals is monitoring student progress, especially as reflected in test scores for each grade, each class, and each student. Such behavior intrinsically reflects an academic focus and academic values. Principals can share results with teachers and elicit agreement on standards. Discrepancies from standards are used to guide corrective action.

5. Principals can acquire material and personnel resources needed for effective instruction and use them creatively in accordance with academic priorities.

6. Principals are responsible for the creation of a safe and orderly school environment. There are many interrelated suggestions regarding the actions principals can take. They can

- Protect teaching and learning time from interruption, for example, by limiting public address system announcements (or classroom phone calls) to specified times; preventing class interruptions by message carriers, other staff, parents, or other visitors; and designing other administrative routines to minimize disruption and distraction.

- Develop clear and consistent policies and promote adherence to rules and regulations. This strategy both directly strengthens orderliness and, more subtly, reinforces the authority and control of teachers (Mackenzie, 1983; Ubben & Hughes, 1987).

- Help teachers learn and use sound principles of classroom management.

- Enlist student participation in creating an orderly and academic environment by creating conditions that allow large numbers of them to participate in, for example, leadership positions, assemblies, school outings, academic clubs, and competitions such as language and computer clubs, bowl games, athletics, pompon teams, Odyssey of the Mind, and Future Problem Solving.

- Maintain an attractive and well-decorated building, which conveys to students the message that the staff cares about a pleasant and academically oriented school environment.

- Express an interest in students' personal well-being, perhaps by inquiring about illnesses or injuries, families, classes, and activities, or even teasing about social lives (Lee, 1987).

- If necessary, discipline, expel, or otherwise deal with habitual intimidators and troublemakers. In 1988 one principal bent on creating an academic school environment repeatedly made national headlines with his controversial action of quickly and simply kicking the so-called bad youngsters out of his school.

7. Principals can monitor other factors known to correlate with achievement, factors that relate to instructional improvement yet implicitly emphasize an academic school climate. For example, effective principals can monitor whether most of the school day is spent in academic engagement, with teachers directly teaching academic skills. They also can note whether lessons are planned in advance, classes and lessons start on time, and teaching and learning proceed without interruption. Principals can support the use of teacher planning and work groups, which leads to better teaching, higher rates of innovation, and higher job satisfaction and feelings of competence.

Principals can help ensure that teachers reward achievement and praise students for work that is well done. They also can monitor whether worthwhile homework assignments, rather than repetitious busywork, are given and ensure that staff are available to help students who have problems.

8. A major instructional function of effective principals is observing teachers in the classroom and conferring with them about ways to deal with problems and improve instruction. Such procedures implicitly convey an academic school orientation and the principal's dedication to improved teaching and higher student achievement. We shall take a closer look at principals' observation and feedback procedures in Chapter 6, along with ideas for teacher observation and peer supervision and teacher work groups and teams.

CHARACTERISTICS OF EFFECTIVE PRINCIPALS

It is impossible to separate characteristics of effective principals from their attitudes, expectations, and actual behavior. Therefore, this description will overlap and continue the previous section's description of behaviors contributing to an academic climate.

In a global description of effective principals, Rutherford (1985) listed essential qualities that have been identified by research clearly and consistently. As we have seen, effective principals have clear and informed visions of what they want their schools to become—visions that focus on students and their needs. These principals translate their visions into goals for the school and expectations for teachers, students, and administrators. They establish a school climate that supports progress toward these goals and expectations.

Good instructional leaders also monitor teaching progress by observing their teachers at work in the classroom and providing feedback after every observation. Less effective principals might say, "My teachers are all professionals, so I leave them alone to do their work." If such principals are required to observe and evaluate, they are likely to give every teacher an average (or perfect) rating or even let the teachers themselves fill in the rating forms.

Rutherford also noted that effective principals intervene in a supportive and positive manner—teachers are praised for good work and positive contributions. When teaching problems arise, these principals provide supportive assistance that produces improvement.

As part of their classic Michigan studies, Brookover, Beady, Flood, and Schweitzer (1979) identified some interesting and suggestive differences among principals of a high-achieving white school, a high-achieving black school, a low-achieving white school, and a low-achieving black school. The findings highlight the characteristics, values, and behaviors of effective and ineffective principals. The principal of the high-achieving, largely white school stated that his primary concern was student achievement. He not only delegated routine paperwork to an assistant but announced that during the year he would observe each teacher in class 30 times—just as he had done the year before. He supported inservice workshops and urged teachers to discuss school and instructional improvements with him. All teachers respected this principal and appreciated his interest in student achievement.

The former principal of the high-achieving, mostly black school, to whom teachers attributed the success of the school, showed most of these same qualities. This principal also was deeply concerned with student achievement. He was an instructional as well as administrative leader and personally conducted many inservice training sessions. In contrast, the current (and less effective) principal of this school "was primarily an effective administrator who kept good records . . . [and] believed that the primary responsibility for the quality of education . . . rested with the teachers" (Good & Brophy, 1985).

What about the two principals of the low-achieving schools? The principal of the low-achieving, mostly white school saw his major responsibility as dealing with student problems. He interacted very little with teachers, rarely observed them in classrooms, had low expectations for student achievement, and spent a lot of time working with problem students and compiling files on them. Similarly, the principal in the ineffective, mostly black school saw herself as an administrator and disciplinarian, not an instructional leader. Although she was interested in student achievement, she spent little time observing or critiquing teachers, and she held low expectations for both students and teachers.

Many other characteristics (skills, knowledge, beliefs, personality traits, behaviors) of effective principals have recurred in the literature. Most of these relate to (a) leadership traits and skills, (b) problem-solving abilities, (c) social skills, or (d) professional knowledge and competence.

Leadership Traits

It has become abundantly clear from research on effective schooling that the leadership of the principal is the single most powerful determinant of school effectiveness. Effective principals

- Have a desire to lead and a willingness to act with courage and deliberation in difficult situations (Little & Bird, 1987).

- Are high in initiative and resourcefulness (Blumberg & Greenfield, 1986).

- Are highly goal-oriented and have a keen sense of clarity regarding instructional and organizational goals (Blumberg & Greenfield, 1986).

- Set good examples by working hard themselves (Ubben & Hughes, 1987).

- Recognize the uniqueness of teachers in their styles, attitudes, skills, and orientations and support different styles of teaching. Effective principals match teaching skills with teaching arrangements and assignments.

- Flexibly schedule demands on staff time.

- Have the ability to let teachers emerge as leaders (Ubben & Hughes, 1987).

- Identify their roles in terms of providing educational leadership and creating an environment for learning. They are less concerned with administrative routine.

- Are aware of the informal dimension of leadership in the school, that is, leadership based upon power (e.g., department heads), prestige, or personality, which may or may not jibe with the formal leadership structure of the school.

- Most important, are proactive rather than reactive—they take charge of the job and do not let the job take charge of them.

As for leadership styles, see the four types described by K. Peterson in Inset 2-1. Note that a principal's appearance of supposed effectiveness—the *problem selector, caretaker,* and *firefighter* styles—can be highly deceptive.

Problem–Solving Abilities

As we saw in the description of a principal's daily activities, the problem-solving and decision-making activities of every principal begin early and run late. Effective principals have a high tolerance for ambiguity and can cope effectively with ambiguous situations (Dwyer, Lee, Rowan, & Bossert, 1983). For example, a principal's decision making can be based upon such criteria as good educational practice, political expediency, friendliness, efficiency, convenience, or others (Greenfield, 1987). Effective principals approach problems from a highly analytic perspective, looking for cause—effect relationships that might suggest solutions.

It is important to note that good principals prefer to include others in problem solving (Blumberg & Greenfield, 1986). Doing so not only helps in analyzing the problem and finding solutions, it also creates ownership of the problem and a commitment to an effective solution. An advantage of greater empowerment of teachers is that the increased problem-solving responsibility dramatically increases their ownership of problems.

Also aiding in problem solving is a communication system that allows information and ideas to "flow up and down the line" (Peterfreund Associates, 1970).

Social Skills

One has only to think about the position of the principal in the school social environment to appreciate the importance of social skills and abilities. The principal must be on friendly terms with

INSET 2–1

Entrepreneurs, Problem Selectors, Caretakers, and Firefighters: Four Leadership Styles

The Instructional Management Program, created at the Far West Laboratory for Educational Research and Development in San Francisco, was a research project focusing on leadership styles of principals. For this project, 17 principals of urban, suburban, and rural schools were selected by their superiors as being effective leaders. The principals, both men and women, were interviewed and followed in their daily work. Kent Peterson (1986), a member of the research team, identified four leadership styles which he labeled *Entrepreneur, Problem Selector, Caretaker*, and *Firefighter*. Each style was related to a combination of the vision of the principal, the problem density of the school environment, and the principal's problem-solving patterns.

Peterson's Entrepreneur is an energetic principal with a strong vision for the direction and goals of the school, which is a relatively smooth-running school with low problem density. The Entrepreneur is a proactive, supportive, and facilitative leader. He or she is visible to teachers, students, and parents; delegates responsibility to teachers and teacher planning groups; and uses shared decision making in solving problems. The Entrepreneur may create heroes among the staff and students, individuals whose behavior reflects values consistent with his or her vision for the school. The focus of the school is on excellence; the staff feel they are professionals; and students feel wanted and encouraged.

The Problem Selector also is a principal with vision but finds himself or herself in a relatively dense problem environment. The Problem Selector tends to focus attention on particular problems that can be solved successfully. While this type of principal appears proactive and effective, the approach leaves many problems ignored, put on hold, or only partially solved.

The Caretaker is a principal with unclear vision in a school with relatively few problems. Because everything seems to run smoothly, the Caretaker's school appears successful and so does the Caretaker. In reality, with little or no attention paid to innovation, program improvement, or staff development, the school is stagnant and declining.

Finally, the Firefighter also has unclear (and seemingly uncorrectable) vision in a school with a high problem density. This principal's strategy is to tackle and instantly solve each problem as it arises. While the Firefighter seems effective—coping quickly and successfully with many school problems—the result of this style often is chaos. The Firefighter wins the short-term battles but with no regard to long-range effects. In fact, the same problems emerge again and again. Important long-range planning for school and teaching improvement becomes impossible. The poor leadership of the Firefighter and the lack of progress toward long-term school improvement may cause teachers to lose respect for this principal, and some may even seek transfers.

In view of the research-based description of an effective principal as one who has a vision for the school, has high expectations of staff and students, observes and coaches teachers, and monitors student progress, Peterson rightfully concluded that of the four types, only the style of the Entrepreneur could truly be considered an effective and desirable approach to school leadership.

---

the school staff, yet maintain leadership authority and earn their respect and willingness to cooperate. The principal also must work with the central office and maintain good relations with parents and others in the community.

It is not a great surprise, then, that effective principals have been found to have high interpersonal competence. That is, they are strong in the social and leadership skills that elicit support and cooperation. They are high in personal security and have a well-developed sense of themselves as individuals (Blumberg & Greenfield, 1986). They tend to possess the personal flexibility to be genuinely themselves whether controlling and directing the activities of others or showing compassion in satisfying the social needs of individual teachers (Ubben & Hughes, 1987).

Effective principals are friendly and good-natured; they go out of their way to help teachers. They also take into account the personality, interests, needs, goals, and ambitions of teachers and other staff. Such traits and goals may or may not be compatible with the goals of the organization, and therefore will dictate which ideas and information will be accepted or rejected. The principal recognizes that the private goals of the individual will directly affect efforts to reach the public goals of the school (Ubben & Hughes, 1987). Therefore, the principal will provide ways to satisfy personal needs and goals within the organization—ways that are consistent with organizational goals.

Professional Knowledge and Competence

Effective principals know and can apply research-based principles of teaching and learning. Effective teaching practices may be modeled or illustrated for the staff by such principals. They consider the implications for teaching and learning when making decisions about schedules, budgets, equipment and supplies, teaching assignments, and the use of faculty meetings. Good principals are in tune with district objectives and integrate them into school goals and educational planning (Peterfreund Associates, 1970).

It will be heartening to learn that, as with vision, effective principals are not necessarily born with the central skills and traits. They can be learned. Three programs designed to improve the effectiveness of principals include the Harvard Principals' Center, Vanderbilt University's 2-week summer institute, and the Peer-Assisted Leadership Program at the Far West Regional Laboratory in San Francisco (Little & Bird, 1987). In one unique study by Gall, Fielding, Schalock, Charters, and Wiczinski (1984), principals were trained to be more effective instructional leaders in accordance with the attitudes and behaviors summarized in this chapter. The training had a positive impact on their teachers' implementation of a mathematics program that produced measurable increases in student achievement.

In Chapter 6 we shall look more closely at a central instructional leadership role of effective principals, classroom observation and instructional supervision. As we shall see, the skills required to observe and provide positive and constructive feedback to teachers—in ways that are both socially acceptable and based upon principles of effective teaching—are indeed learnable. For example, we shall examine how the Beloit, Wisconsin, Public School System is training its principals to (a) create a collegial atmosphere in which classroom observation is accepted as worthwhile and positive and (b) carry out the observation and supervision in a nonthreatening and supportive manner.

INSTRUCTIONAL LEADERSHIP FROM A WHY, WHAT, AND HOW PERSPECTIVE

Achilles (1987) described how the vision and leadership of effective principals can be reduced to the three basic questions of *why, what,* and *how:* Effective principals must know why better education is needed, what is needed to improve schools, and how to administer their schools to achieve the best results.

The *why* questions relate to vision—the tendency of effective principals to envision and work toward what their schools can become. Some good why questions grew out of early research with highly successful low-SES schools: Why were these schools successful? Why couldn't students in other schools experience the same achievement and success?

The *what* questions follow on the heels of *why.* What is going on in effective schools? What are the common elements among different effective schools? What can we do to achieve successful school outcomes?

We have seen much of the what and how of effective schooling, and more will be addressed in later chapters. For now, we shall look at additional specifics of what principals can do and how they can do it to increase the effectiveness of their schools.

Achilles, describing project SHAL (the initials refer to four participant schools), summarized the what and how of instructional leadership in three sequential levels, corresponding to the 3 years of SHAL implementation.

In the first level (year), the principal largely orients the school staff to the changes and begins implementing preliminary steps. Specifically, the principal

- Accepts responsibility for what goes on at school. For principals who have focused on administration and discipline, leaving teaching to teachers, this step requires a substantial change in outlook.

- Establishes goals and sets norms based on policy expectations of the district, community values, and his or her own vision of an excellent school.

- Focuses efforts on instruction and begins classroom visits.

- Develops activities and structure consistent with the goals, norms, and purposes of education.

- Remakes schedules to support uninterrupted learning blocks, teacher planning time, and so forth.

- Fosters open communication, decision-making, and problem-solving channels. Seeks to establish a collegial atmosphere.

- Focuses faculty meetings on solving problems.

- Plans an academic emphasis and orientation.

- Plans structures that reward achievement by both students and staff.

- Initiates community awareness and involvement.

In the second level (year), the principal proceeds with still more concrete action that implements the ideas and orientations of the first year. The principal

- Emphasizes an academic school climate, high expectations, an emphasis on basic skills, assessment of progress, and student achievement. Staff interest is focused on these.

- Strives to establish a school-wide sense of community.

- Transmits the vision of an excellent school to the staff, students, and parents.

- Moves from a narrow problem focus to a broader program orientation.

- Becomes even more visible in the hallways, classrooms, school grounds, and community.

- Initiates regular classroom observation and instructional supervision sessions.

- Schedules instructional training events (e.g., inservice workshops on effective schools and effective teachers).

- Provides ongoing support to staff while focusing on larger school goals.

- Becomes better acquainted with the school community, including staff, pupils, parents, and the neighborhood; treats staff, students, parents, and others with respect.

In the third level (final year), the principal takes final steps in implementing changes in the school climate and procedures and fine-tunes the ongoing reforms. The principal

- Continues to set and transmit personal and school-wide goals and objectives that are in agreement with district policy.
- Monitors the instructional process and programs.
- Coordinates instructional programs, continuing to emphasize achievement.
- Takes an assertive role in program development and evaluation and decisions about selecting instructional materials.
- Plans and schedules to make optimal use of material and personnel resources.
- Organizes teacher inservice training in both specific content areas and classroom management techniques.
- Keeps abreast of relevant research and ideas for effective leadership, effective schools, and effective instruction.
- Refines standards of performance for teachers, pupils, and self.

Improving school effectiveness—which includes making the pivotal changes in climate, staff expectations, and student self-expectations; installing acceptable classroom observation and supervision strategies; and developing teacher and administration evaluation and monitoring procedures—can hardly occur overnight. Some experts estimate that 5 years is a prudent period for such school-wide changes in attitudes and procedures. Achilles's 3-year plan and schedule, while appearing optimistic, has proved successful. Interested readers are encouraged to see Achilles (1987) for further details.

COMMENTARY

We have three final comments regarding the complexity of the principal's role in creating a more effective school. First, one sobering reminder by Purkey and Smith (1982) and Greenfield

(1987) is that, although great strides obviously have been made, the construct of instructional leadership remains ambiguous. In fact, despite the existence of training programs and descriptive literature, some claim that the art of instructional leadership does not yet exist. Further, evidence for a direct cause–effect relationship between the efforts of school principals and the accomplishments of teachers and students is not as clear as we would like. For example, few experimental studies have been carried out that unambiguously demonstrate that training a principal causes teacher performance and student achievement to improve measurably. However, it seems likely that clear direction and concrete action of the variety described in this chapter, carried out by a principal with vision, will promote growth toward school and teaching effectiveness. Purkey and Smith (1982), Greenfield (1987), Lipham (1981), Sergiovanni (1987), Ubben and Hughes (1987), and many others agree that schools can be improved and that principals play a key role in that improvement.

Second, while this chapter has summarized some universal traits and leadership behaviors that both research and intuition indicate usually characterize an effective principal, there is no one ideal style of good leadership by principals. For example, in a study by Hall, Hord, Huling, Rutherford, and Stiegelbauer (1983), different principals were found to use different leadership styles, yet all were effective. In the terminology of Hall and his colleagues, the *initiators* would "make it happen," the *managers* would "help it happen," and the *responders* would "let it happen." Most of this chapter has focused on the initiator, the make-it-happen principal, and to a lesser degree the manager, who by empowering teachers will help it happen.

As we saw in Inset 2-1, seemingly effective leadership styles can, in fact, be quite ineffective. Peterson's (1986) Caretaker style might be judged by parents, the school board, and even teachers as effective because the school runs smoothly. Never mind about innovation or reform. Problem Selectors can be perceived as effective because they actively and visibly solve selected problems; however, they leave many unsolved. Firefighters are easily seen as effective because they deal with short-term problems quickly and smartly; but this is at the expense of long-term planning. Of Peterson's four styles, only the Entrepreneur style—the proactive, supportive, and visionary principal who creates a collegial climate and empowers teachers to improve school excellence—is truly effective.

The third comment is that the SES level of the community and other context factors will strongly affect a school's mission, values, and goals and therefore the principal's vision and leadership efforts. For example, Hallinger and Murphy (1987) noted that parents in lower SES schools favor emphases on social and vocational goals, while upper SES parents stress academics. Note also that effective low-SES schools have focused instruction on improving basic reading and mathematics skills, while effective high-SES schools pursue a more broadly defined mission (Brookover & Lezotte, 1979). Principals also must behave in ways that are comfortable to the community and consistent with the policies of the school board, superintendent, and teachers' union if, as Burlingame (1987) euphemistically put it, "they expect to stay in their roles." The principal clearly must develop a mission consistent with the school's social and educational context.

SUMMARY

Strong instructional leadership by a principal with vision is the single most critical component of a successful, effective school. Such principals have high achievement expectations, observe teachers teaching, and monitor individual and collective student achievement.

The work of the principal is "varied, brief, and fragmented" (Martin & Willower, 1981), largely verbal, and very busy as he or she monitors work operations; supervises; dispenses information; allocates resources; serves as spokesperson; implements educational ideas; deals with safety, orderliness, and conflict; and keeps things going as peacefully as possible (Blumberg, 1987). Based on his analyses of principals' activities and responsibilities, Blumberg concluded that the work is a highly skilled craft.

Effective principals tend to be energetic and have working theories that guide their actions. Their focus is on *instructional leadership,* which refers to actions that develop a productive and satisfying work environment for teachers and promote growth in student learning.

A principal's leadership role could conflict with the notion of empowering teachers. However, when the principal is viewed as a manager of experts, leadership is shared and all work together for school improvement.

An effective principal's vision of what a school can be guides the setting of goals and objectives, the assessment of how well the school is functioning, and other actions geared to instructional improvement. The principal's vision is transmitted to the school staff. Ineffective principals tend not to possess such vision, but it can be developed by learning about and visiting effective schools.

Effective principals are instrumental in creating a strong sense of community, an academically oriented school climate, high expectations for student achievement, and caring about young people. An organizational culture—consistent values, rules, and goals—holds the school together.

Among many suggestions for creating an academic climate (or culture), the principal can

- Raise awareness of and gain consensus for school improvements and higher achievement expectations.
- Take an active role in school improvement strategies.
- Create motivational devices and reward systems that support an academic orientation.
- Monitor academic progress.
- Use material and personnel resources creatively.
- Maintain a safe, orderly, and pleasant environment.
- Monitor teaching practices.
- Observe and provide feedback on teaching.

Some specifics that promote the development of an academic climate include ensuring that academic engagement rates are high; classes start on time and proceed without interruption; meaningful homework is assigned; lessons are planned in advance; course planning is conducted by teacher groups; and staff are available to help students.

Recurrent characteristics of effective principals center on their strong vision, which influences setting goals for the school; high expectations for teachers, students, and other staff; and monitoring progress.

Brookover's research with two high-achieving and two low-achieving schools confirmed the importance of principals' instructional leadership in the form of concern for achievement, holding high expectations, observing and coaching teachers, supporting staff development, and related qualities.

Many characteristics of effective principals fall into the four categories of strong leadership skills and traits, effective problem-solving and decision-making abilities, high social skills, and good professional knowledge and competence.

Peterson described four leadership styles: Entrepreneur, Problem Selector, Caretaker, and Firefighter. While all were *perceived* as effective, only the Entrepreneur style was truly effective.

Principals can learn to be more effective instructional leaders, for example, in training programs that stress behaviors and attitudes described in this chapter and teach classroom observation and supervision techniques.

Achilles described instructional leadership in terms of why better schooling is needed, what is needed to improve schools, and how to administer a school for best results. Based on project SHAL, Achilles summarized a 3-year plan for instructional improvement.

The construct of instructional leadership remains ambiguous. There is no one ideal leadership style. A school's SES level, the superintendent and school board, and other context factors will influence the principal's vision and leadership efforts.

Experts agree that schools can be improved and that principals play a key role in this improvement.

Chapter Three

Effective Schools

The amount of agreement on the principal factors in school effectiveness is so striking that the question of what is important in school effectiveness may now be less significant than the question of what can be changed for the least cost and the most results.
—Donald E. Mackenzie, "Research for School Improvement: An Appraisal of Some Recent Trends"

One of the cardinal characteristics of effective schools is that they are as eager to avoid things that don't work as they are committed to implementing things that do.
—Ronald R. Edmonds, "Effective Schools for the Urban Poor"

Much of the same research and many of the same findings are interpreted from the different perspectives of effective schools, effective principals, and effective teaching. For example, in Chapter 2 we suggested that effective principals encourage and monitor such teacher practices as using instructional time efficiently, implementing new instructional approaches, using good curriculum materials, starting and ending classes on time, keeping learning free from interruption, assigning homework, planning in teacher groups, and being available to students. Are these also characteristics of effective schools? Effective teachers?

While school, principal, and teacher variables are intermixed, the differences nonetheless justify looking at effective schooling from each perspective. Chapter 2 examined the crucial role of a dynamic principal in creating and monitoring conditions associated with school success. This chapter reviews other characteristics of effective schools including school-wide climate and policies, effects of leadership, teacher patterns and behaviors, and some classroom management principles. Chapter 4 further explores classroom management techniques, while Chapter 5 continues with the teacher's viewpoint in looking more closely at specific teaching strategies as well as classroom characteristics and patterns associated with high achievement and good school attitudes. Chapter 6 reviews classroom observation and coaching by the principal and by fellow teachers, along with advantages of teacher work groups.

Only a few years ago Bickel (1983) outlined three elementary but central assumptions of the effective-schools movement, assumptions that, based on research, reflect our optimism about teaching children. First, there *are* schools that are unusually successful in teaching poor and minority children basic skills, as evaluated by standardized tests. Second, these effective schools share characteristics that are correlated with their success, characteristics that are well within the domain of educators to manipulate. Finally, these characteristics provide a basis for improving currently unsuccessful schools. Actually, Bickel underestimated the impact of effective-schools research; the characteristics it has revealed are providing an important part of the basis for educational reform and school improvement programs nation-wide.

Chapter 1 included a description of several background issues, problems, and complications to help readers take a more informed look at research on effective schools. This chapter next provides some additional inside-view issues and cautions.

COMPARING EFFECTIVE
WITH INEFFECTIVE SCHOOLS

Many studies of effective schools have taken a comparative approach. They have identified schools matched on SES that are highly effective and notably ineffective, and then have searched for characteristics that might account for the difference. Klitgaard and Hall (1974) and Purkey and Smith (1983) argued that it would be more logical to compare both the effective and ineffective schools with *average* schools. What interests us is discovering what characteristics make certain schools better or worse than average schools; that is, what makes them *outliers*. Also, the key differences between effective and average schools may be quite unlike the differences between effective and ineffective schools. In a practical sense, poor schools are more likely to benefit by understanding why they are below average rather than knowing how they compare with outstanding schools (Purkey & Smith, 1983).

SOCIOECONOMIC LEVEL AND EFFECTIVENESS

It is well known that average school achievement is closely related to the socioeconomic level of the students. Therefore, researchers have been careful to compare effective and ineffective schools that lie within the same SES level. It would do little good to conclude that teacher and principal expectations are significantly higher and the academic climate is better in the school for high-SES super-achievers than in the school for low-SES children of lower ability.

There are several concerns regarding the stratifying strategy. First, there could be errors in the assessment of social class and home background or in the statistical regression formulas used by some researchers to identify outlier schools from large masses of data (e.g., Fetler & Carlson, 1985; Klitgaard & Hall, 1974). If errors exist, differences in effectiveness will be inextricably tangled with SES level. Leadership, climate, or teaching variables associated with school success cannot be isolated when the overwhelming and overriding factor is community SES and educational level.

Second, a supposedly effective school serving mostly low-income and minority students may show achievement scores that, in fact, are below the average of middle-class schools (e.g., Armor et al., 1976). Therefore, even an average suburban school may possess important advantages over a so-called effective lower SES school—advantages and characteristics that will be ignored in descriptions of effective outlier schools.

Third, characteristics of low-SES schools that are described as effective may have limited generalizability to middle-class schools. That is, because middle-class students already are likely to be achieving at good levels, principles for raising achievement in these schools may be different from principles and strategies for increasing achievement in low-SES schools.

MOST RESEARCH HAS BEEN IN ELEMENTARY SCHOOLS

One frequently cited problem is that most research on effective schools not only has been conducted in low-SES schools, it also has involved elementary rather than secondary schools (Cuban, 1983; Firestone & Herriot, 1982; Good & Brophy, 1985; Sizer, 1985; Van Der Burg, 1986). There are important differences between elementary and secondary schools in school organization, teachers, and students that may affect variables claimed to improve school effectiveness.

Elementary teachers form more of a work group. Therefore, it is much easier both for a principal to exert influence and for teachers to agree on a common focus such as basic skills at this level. In secondary schools the departmental organization is more complex. Different departments emphasize different goals, and teachers are subject-matter specialists. Because there are more layers of administration in secondary schools, school improvement leadership is more likely to take a team form. For example, a principal or an assistant principal may form a leadership group with one or more department heads.

Students also differ between elementary and secondary schools in more ways than just size, shape, and educational level. Young children often adore their teachers and have good school attitudes while secondary students vary dramatically in their attitudes and values regarding school and teachers. Strong peer norms can support cooperation, achievement, and eventual career success or else drugs, alcohol, crime, and an adversarial "us against them" attitude.

Bondi and Wiles (1986) described almost comically some differences among middle-school students, some of which may bear on efforts to improve school attitudes and achievement. According to them, a 13-year-old youngster may be 6 feet tall or 4 feet 7; trip on stairs or win Olympic gold medals in gymnastics; be an alcoholic or drug addict or a Sunday school teacher; wear braces or compete in Miss Teenage America contests; be turned off and looking forward to quitting school or a curious and enthusiastic learner; be unable to read comic strips or read *The Wall Street Journal*; have trouble with whole numbers or be able to solve geometry problems; appear regularly in juvenile court or be an Eagle Scout; be a mother or father or still play with dolls or toy cars.

Educators must use caution in extending findings from research at the elementary level to the secondary school setting.

DO ONE OR TWO GRADES
EQUAL A SCHOOL?

As the research details that follow will show, researchers who study effective schools rarely include the entire school (Rowan, Bossert, & Dwyer, 1983). Rather, they often study just one or two grade levels and evaluate achievement in one or two subjects, virtually always reading and/or mathematics. There is a tremendous growth in reading ability in grades one to three and usually a dramatic drop in reading scores from sixth to seventh grade. Researchers who evaluate sixth-grade reading might reach quite different conclusions if they selected seventh-graders in the same school. Generally, the danger is that dynamics of effectiveness uncovered for one grade or one subject may not be relevant to other grades or other subjects.

CAUSAL ORDERING

We noted in Chapter 1 that most research has been observational and case study research and correlational research. These approaches establish relationships between student achievement on one hand and leadership, climate, and teaching factors on the other. An experimental study, in which an experimental group of teachers or principals is trained in a leadership or teaching technique while a control group is not, permits researchers to more clearly establish what factors do, in fact, cause the higher achievement. Unfortunately, experimental studies are rare, no doubt because they are more difficult and expensive to conduct.

The problem of establishing causation should be of concern to anyone interested in the effective-schooling literature. Too many of the major findings could, with only a little imagination, be interpreted in several ways: Factor 1 may indeed cause factor 2, factor 2 may cause factor 1, or both factors 1 and 2 may be caused by factor 3, which was not studied at all. The easiest example of this is the very common finding that the administration, staff, and students in effective schools all hold strong expectations for high achievement. Do the high expectations cause the higher achievement, as is assumed? Or does the high level of student achievement lead everyone to hold optimistic expectations? Or are both the expectations and the achievement caused by a third factor, perhaps academic, family, and community values? The differences are important, because the first interpretation implies that taking steps to change staff and student expectations will have a beneficial effect on achievement, while the latter two interpretations do not. It makes little sense to incorporate changes that are consequences, not causes, of school improvement.

Rowan, Bossert, and Dwyer (1983) presented other pertinent examples. As we saw in Chapter 2, effective schools almost always have a principal who is a strong instructional leader, which suggests that we can improve school effectiveness by training principals in instructional leadership. An alternate interpretation, however, is that effectiveness and good leadership might be attributed to the principal because he or she heads a highly effective organization. That is, principal leadership might follow, instead of preceding, school effectiveness. As a related example, the finding that principals of effective schools spend more time in the classroom observing and evaluating teachers might be due to their having more competent teachers—teachers who are more willing to allow principals to observe and evaluate them and who seek professional improvement.

Most often, it is accurate to assume that causation is in the apparently reasonable direction. That is, principal and teacher attitudes and behaviors in a particular school do indeed cause the improved student attitudes and achievement. Based on this assumption, for example, the U.S. Department of Education (1986, 1987) prepared its well-received booklet, *What Works: Research About Teaching and Learning*. However, the informed reader should be aware that in some cases an alternate explanation is at least possible and that the interrelationships always are complicated. As Rowan, Bossert, and Dwyer (1983) put it, "Factors such as leadership, expectations, and effectiveness are related by a pattern of simultaneous causation that defies simple description."

IDENTIFYING EFFECTIVENESS IS NOT THE SAME AS CREATING EFFECTIVENESS

Most research only *describes* currently effective schools. However, identifying characteristics of effective schools is not the same as creating an effective school environment.

Rowan, Bossert, and Dwyer (1983) provocatively suggested that high achievement actually might cause school effectiveness, rather than the reverse. That is, students with higher motivation and higher levels of achievement, due perhaps to family and peer values, make the school's existing policies and procedures—regardless of what they are—look effective.

D'Amico (1982) offered a related idea, suggesting that each successful school might be composed of a unique and highly idiosyncratic combination of administrators, teachers, and students. If this is the case, according to D'Amico, an effective school can be a model "only for itself" and cannot be duplicated.

These two perspectives, while interesting, are off base. Student achievement *has* been improved by training principals and teachers in leadership, teaching, and management behaviors known to correlate with high achievement. For example, in Chapter 2 we reviewed a successful three-level training program for principals that was designed to improve school effectiveness (Achilles, 1987). Gall and colleagues (1984) installed a successful training program for principals that also improved teacher performance and student mathematics achievement. Evertson, Anderson, Anderson, and Brophy (1980) successfully improved teachers' classroom management skills based on strategies found by research to be effective. Two other projects, Milwaukee's Project Rise (McCormack-Larkin & Kritek, 1983) and the New York City School Improvement Project (Clark & McCarthy, 1983), described later in this chapter, also successfully incorporated characteristics of effective schools. In fact, as we noted earlier, research-based characteristics of effective schools are guiding educational reform and teaching improvement plans in every state (e.g., Mack, 1988).

DIFFERENCES AMONG STUDENT SUBGROUPS

In Chapter 1 we explained the difference between central (general) tendencies and variability in effective-schooling research. Most research does indeed investigate average achievement levels for the entire student body, a practice that hides differences among student subgroups (Airasian, Kellaghan, & Madaus, 1979; Purkey & Smith, 1983). There are ethnic, geographic, or socioeconomic groups within individual schools whose achievement differs from the school average, with *average* often meaning *white middle class.* Conclusions about supposedly important variables associated with average achievement in one school may not apply to these subgroups, nor to other schools composed largely of students from the same subgroups.

In one school district, for example, subgroup differences are built into a mastery-based effective-school program. Based on a concept of *disaggregate data,* mastery goals are adjusted for students from different SES levels (defined by participation or nonparticipation in the free lunch program), with program success defined as meeting these different mastery levels.

SIZE OF SCHOOL EFFECTS

Several researchers have taken a close statistical look at (a) the obtained differences in average achievement between outlier schools selected as effective and those identified as ineffective and (b) the average actual effect of school differences on individual student achievement. Looking at the first issue, it is a statistical fact that if schools are selected because they are outliers—extremely effective or ineffective —some of that difference will be due to random error. That is, on another day or using another measure, the schools would not differ quite so dramatically. Based on achievement data for sixth-graders in 405 California schools, Rowan and Denk (1982) and Rowan, Bossert, and Dwyer (1983) estimated that about 50% of the difference in achievement between effective and ineffective outlier schools was due to real differences in school factors and about 50% was due to random error. The upshot is that when schools are selected as highly effective or ineffective, due to chance factors in measurement they actually are not quite as different as they appear to be.

Let us turn to the second point, the actual effects of school differences on individual student achievement. When various factors were sorted out statistically, Rowan, Bossert, and Dwyer (1983) estimated that only about 4.5% of the differences in individual student achievement are due to school differences. If this estimate is even close to accurate—and it seems very low—it might appear that differences between schools do not make much difference. Indeed, as we saw in Chapter 1, Coleman and his supporters (Jencks et al., 1972) treated school differences as trivial. However, as Gage (1985) pointed out, when we are talking about "drop out rates, literacy, placement in special classes, love of learning, [and] self-esteem . . . differences do not need to be large to be important." Rowan, Bossert, and Dwyer (1983) agreed with "the emerging consensus that school-to-school differences in achievement are significant and worthy of both study and action."

Certainly, the impact of school-effectiveness research on current educational reform programs suggests that few reformers believe school effects to be trivial. Further, when school-effectiveness measures are combined with improvements in teaching and management effectiveness (see Chapters 4, 5, and 6), effects on individual student achievement are likely to be considerably greater than 4.5%.

THERE IS NO ONE RECIPE
FOR EFFECTIVENESS

One final caution is that there is no single combination of variables that can be used to improve the effectiveness of every school (Brookover et al., 1979). There is no simple recipe or easy-to-assemble model (Purkey & Smith, 1983). Although there are indeed marvelous and enlightening consistencies in the research, every single study, in fact, has produced a list of characteristics of successful schools that both overlaps with and differs from the results of every other study.

It would be surprising indeed if all lists of characteristics of effective teachers, principals, and schools were identical and if they applied across the board to all schools. Edmonds (1979) noted, "What effective schools share is a climate in which it is incumbent on all personnel to be instructionally effective for all pupils." However, referring to schools for poor children, Edmonds explained that such a favorable climate might originate in (a) a tyrant principal who compels teachers to bring all children to a minimum level of basic skill mastery, (b) dedicated teachers who are committed to being effective for all children, or (c) a tough-minded parent–teacher organization that holds the school accountable for student achievement. According to Edmonds, "No one model explains school effectiveness for the poor or any other social class subset."

In sum, research on effective schools may be mildly haunted by philosophical or methodological specters. However, almost no one recommends trashing the movement. Probably all researchers in this area agree that schools—their structure, organization, leadership, climate, values, policies, and practices—have an important impact on student achievement. Further, as we will see, recurrent findings are a source of strong and validated suggestions that can help any school become more effective.

STUDIES OF EFFECTIVE SCHOOLS

There are two approaches to describing principles and characteristics of effective schools. We could skip the dreary research details and present what appear to be the main findings of the major studies, as Squires, Huitt, and Segars (1983) and Blum (1984) have done. Or, we could explain the actual procedures and main conclusions of observational research, cases studies, correlational research, experimental studies, and program evaluations as done by Good and Brophy (1985), Purkey and Smith (1983), and Edmonds (1979).

We have chosen to do both. In view of the greater depth of understanding that might be reaped from descriptive accounts of this research, we will look at four historically prominent research projects. This will be followed by a list of specific findings, principles, and recommendations that have surfaced from these four studies and others.

Four Effective Inner–City Schools

One of the first studies of school effectiveness, and certainly the most widely cited, is the case study analysis of four inner-city schools by Weber (1971). His research was in direct response to the popularized conclusions of the Coleman Report, namely, that low social class, low income, low exposure to books, low needs for achievement, and inadequate models comprised a sufficient explanation of the failure of poor children to achieve adequately. Weber chose reading ability as the criterion of school success because an inability to read well denies students access to the professional world and forces them into low-paying jobs or even unemployment. As we saw in Chapter 1, not only is reading ability critical, it also is readily measured.

Weber spent 1 year carefully identifying exemplary elementary schools by asking school officials, publishers, and reading specialists to nominate those that were successful in teaching reading. From an initial pool of 95 that were nominated, 17 schools in seven large cities met the three criteria of being an inner-city school, having a successful reading program, and having a principal willing to participate in the study.

After further evaluation with his own 32-item, 15-minute test of ability to read simple American English, Weber eliminated six schools on the reading success criterion. Another seven were eliminated for failing the inner-city criterion, leaving four inner-city schools that were attended by very poor children yet had successful reading programs. The median third-grade reading scores of all four schools equaled or surpassed the national average, and the percentages of nonreaders were unusually low for such schools.

Weber cautiously conceded that individual schools do many things differently; thus it is impossible to be absolutely certain which characteristics are responsible for the superior reading achievement of these four schools over other inner-city schools. Nonetheless, he cited the following eight characteristics as contributors to the success of their reading programs:

1. Strong leadership, which in one school came from the district superintendent. The leaders were instrumental in setting the tone (climate) of the schools, helping plan instructional strategies, and organizing and distributing the schools' resources to facilitate academic goals.

2. High expectations, which Weber noted are not sufficient for school success but definitely are necessary.

3. An atmosphere of order, purposefulness, pleasantness, pleasure in learning, and relative quiet.

4. A strong emphasis on reading skill acquisition.

5. Careful and frequent evaluations of student progress.

6. The use of phonics.

7. Individualized instruction in the sense of having a high concern for each student's progress and, if necessary, modifying a child's assignments (not in the narrow sense of guiding each child independently).

8. The use of additional reading personnel.

Effective-schooling leader Ronald Edmonds (1979) later chose not to "endorse or pursue" the final three factors (phonics, individualization, additional reading personnel) "because subse-

quent research does not sustain their relevance as it does leadership, expectations, atmosphere, reading emphasis, and assessment." The remaining characteristics (1–5 on the list) virtually duplicate Edmonds's (1979, 1982) model, which some schools have successfully adopted to improve their instructional effectiveness (e.g., Clark & McCarthy, 1983; McCormack-Larkin & Kritek, 1983).

Weber also identified some factors that were not as important: small class size, achievement grouping, and physical facilities (no building was new; two were very old). It helps to know what does *not* count.

Weber revisited two of the schools 2 years later, discovering that one had slightly increased its effectiveness while the other had deteriorated and could no longer be classified as effective. The lesson is that conditions of effectiveness may be temporary; they may change as principals, teachers, or student cohorts change (Good & Brophy, 1985).

By way of criticism, Purkey and Smith (1983) and Good and Brophy (1985) noted that Weber should have included a comparison group of less successful schools to help validate each of these characteristics of effectiveness. That is, he did not ascertain whether less successful schools might have been doing some of the same things. Good and Brophy further noted that Weber failed to explain exactly why the one school program deteriorated, which could have been enlightening.

On the positive side, Weber's early study confirmed that effective schools did indeed exist, and he inspired many followers to search for characteristics of successful schools. As we will see, his own list—especially the characteristics of leadership, expectations, atmosphere, emphasis on the basics, and monitoring progress—has withstood the test of time as a guide to the core traits of effective schools.

Search for Effective Schools

The late Ronald R. Edmonds also is a recognized pioneer in the effective-schooling movement. His landmark Search for Effective Schools project produced a short but influential list of characteristics that have been guideposts for many school improvement programs (see Inset 3-1).

Edmonds (1979, 1982) and Lezotte, Edmonds, and Ratner (1974) again studied schools serving poor, mostly minority, inner-city children, this time in Detroit, Michigan. The first phase of

INSET 3-1

Two School Improvement Programs: Milwaukee's Project Rise and the New York City School Improvement Project

Two major and successful school improvement programs have been built around the recommendations of effective-school leader Ronald Edmonds and others. McCormack-Larkin and Kritek's (1983) Milwaukee Project Rise focused on 18 elementary and 2 middle schools that scored lowest in the city on achievement tests. There were three basic assumptions: First, virtually all students can acquire the basic skills, regardless of race, SES level, or family background. Second, inappropriate school expectations, norms, and practices have caused the underachievement of many minority and poor students. Third, research on effective schools and teaching has identified expectations, norms, policies, and practices associated with high achievement. These three assumptions were operationalized in the following eight features to be implemented:

1. The belief among faculty and students that all students can learn and that the school is primarily responsible for their learning.

2. A strong sense of academic mission.

3. Grade-level expectations and standards in reading, mathematics, and language.

4. An accelerated learning program for students performing well below grade level, which included whole-class grade-level instruction plus small-group instruction at the students' actual skill levels.

5. Increased active student learning time (time on task, academic engagement).

6. A high level of professional collegiality among staff members.

7. A strong sense of student identification and affiliation with the school.

8. A structured learning environment.

(continued)

After 3 years there were strong improvements in mathematics scores and good, although less dramatic, improvements in reading, both measured by the Metropolitan Achievement Tests (MAT). In mathematics, the third-grade MAT scores increased from 56 to 82 (city average = 84) and the fifth-grade scores increased from 58 to 79 (city average = 83). In reading, the third-grade scores increased from 53 to 64 (city average = 77) and the fifth-grade scores increased from 45 to 58 (city average = 71).

The New York School Improvement Project (SIP) (Clark & McCarthy, 1983) also based their program on Edmonds's (1979) assumption that schools can educate all children regardless of family background. The following five factors identified by Edmonds and others as core contributors to school success guided the program:

1. Strong administrative and instructional leadership.

2. High teacher expectations along with behaviors that convey those expectations.

3. An academic school climate.

4. Instructional emphasis on basic skills.

5. Continuing assessment of pupil progress.

The results showed that the percentage of students reading at or above grade level, as measured by the California Achievement Tests, increased much more in SIP schools compared with the city-wide average of other New York City schools.

Some schools were more successful than others in stimulating improvements in reading achievement. Confirming the significance of strong instructional leadership, Good and Brophy (1985) said of the New York School Improvement Project, "In schools where the plan worked the principals supervised and coordinated implementation of the plan components and monitored results closely."

Edmonds's research aimed merely at confirming that instructionally effective schools for poor children did, in fact, exist. Briefly, reading and mathematics scores from the Iowa Test of Basic Skills and the Stanford Achievement Test were used to identify which of

20 inner-city schools scored at or above city-wide averages and which scored below. Two schools were matched on the basis of no less than 11 economic, family, and community factors. One school averaged nearly 4 months above the city average in both reading and mathematics, while the other school averaged nearly 3 months below the city average in reading and 1.5 months below the city average in mathematics. With such careful matching on social indicators, there was excellent reason to argue that the differences in achievement were, in fact, due to school characteristics. The concept of instructionally effective schools was no myth.

In the second phase, Edmonds aimed at identifying characteristics of successful schools. Turning from the 20 Detroit schools, Edmonds and his colleagues (e.g., Frederickson, 1975) re-analyzed data from the 1966 Equal Educational Opportunity Survey (EEOS)—the data from which Coleman and his colleagues concluded that schools themselves have little effect on student achievement, compared with nonschool factors. From this large data base, and despite Coleman's famous conclusion, 55 schools were identified as instructionally effective when students' family background and home environment were controlled (e.g., parents' education, parents' occupation, percentage of white students, family size, and percentage of intact families).

One finding pertains to our earlier point that average school achievement may not apply to subgroups within the school. Edmonds reported that some schools were consistently effective in teaching some subgroups of children but were not consistently effective in teaching others. According to Edmonds (1979), the important subgroup differences determining whether a school was effective or not were principally economic and social, not racial.

Based on his own research, the re-analysis of the EEOS data, and a literature review, Edmonds proposed that effective schools

1. Have strong instructional leadership, without which the elements of good schools cannot be created nor held together.

2. Have a climate of academic expectations in which all personnel seek to be instructionally effective for all students and no children are permitted to fall below minimum levels of achievement.

3. Have an atmosphere that is "orderly without being rigid, quiet without being oppressive, and generally conducive to the instructional business at hand."

4. Make it clear that the acquisition of basic skills takes precedence over all other school activities.

5. If necessary, divert energy and resources from other business to further the fundamental objectives.

6. Frequently monitor student progress by either classroom tests or system-wide standardized tests in order to relate pupil progress to instructional objectives.

Edmonds concluded that "in and of itself, pupil family background neither causes nor precludes elementary school instructional effectiveness."

This and similar strongly worded statements by Edmonds regarding the educability of poor and minority children stand in sharp contrast to other analyses of the EEOS data, analyses that led to the conclusion that differences in achievement are only minimally related to differences in school characteristics. Such a pessimistic conclusion has the effect of blaming children for their poor achievement, thus absolving educators of responsibility for low achievement and relieving them of instructional obligations.

By way of comment, the validity and durability of Weber's and Edmonds's conclusions are evidenced by the following summary list of characteristics of effective schools in the U.S. Department of Education (1986) report, *What Works: Research About Teaching and Learning,* prepared by Herbert Walberg and others:

Vigorous instructional leadership.

A principal who makes clear, consistent, and fair decisions.

Teachers with high expectations that all their students can and will learn.

An emphasis on discipline and a safe and orderly environment.

Instructional practices that focus on basic skills and instructional achievement.

Collegiality among teachers in support of student achievement.

Frequent review of student progress.

Michigan Studies

Additional cornerstone projects are the studies by Brookover and his colleagues (Brookover, Beady, Flood, Schweitzer, & Wisenbaker, 1979; Brookover et al., 1982; Brookover & Lezotte, 1979), which are part *process–product* research and part case studies. As the name suggests, process–product research attempts to relate school processes (inputs) to student outcomes (outputs).

The large-scale, statistically based, process–product portion of the research by Brookover and his colleagues (1979) unfortunately did not produce much in the way of enlightening characteristics of effective schools. They administered questionnaires to a large sample of principals, teachers, and students in grades four and five. Achievement data were obtained from the Michigan School Assessment Reports. The input variables were:

1. Student body composition (average SES level, percentage of white students).

2. School social structure, which included allowing students to talk and work together, time allocations (e.g., academic or administrative), differentiation in students' programs (e.g., using student interests in planning instruction), parent involvement, and teachers' satisfaction with the school structure.

3. School climate, comprised of staff and student perceptions of norms, expectations, and other beliefs and feelings about the school.

The output variables included academic achievement (reading and mathematics), student self-concepts of academic ability, and student self-reliance.

Unfortunately, most differences in average school achievement (output) could not be attributed unambiguously to individual input variables. The main problem was that the input variables—student body composition, school social structure, and school climate—were hopelessly intercorrelated, preventing any conclusions about separate effects. Complex social system characteristics, according to Brookover and his colleagues, were more related to the outputs than were the individual input variables they identified. They further conceded that their analysis could not identify which social system variable or set of variables had the largest impact on achievement in all schools. Good and Brophy (1985) said of the Brookover project that it was "a comprehensive and successful attempt to illustrate that school inputs do not predict student outcomes (achievement, self-concept, self-reliance) independent of school processes."

A more enlightening supplement to the large-scale statistical approach of Brookover and his colleagues was their case study observations and interviews in four of the low-SES inner-city schools they studied. Two of the schools were mostly black and two mostly white, with one school in each pair being effective and the other ineffective. *Effectiveness* and *ineffectiveness* were defined as mean achievement scores above or below the average of the large sample, respectively. Each school was visited for a period of 3 weeks to 4 months. Teachers and students in grades one through six were studied.

While there were variations among all four schools, as there would be among any set of four schools, the interesting and pertinent comparisons are between the two effective versus the two ineffective schools, which produced another often-cited list of characteristics of successful schools. In the effective mostly white and mostly black schools,

1. Most of the school day was spent on instruction. While students worked, teachers were available for clarification and reteaching. (In contrast, and due to low expectations, teachers in the low-achieving schools spent as little as 10% of the class time on instruction. Low-level tasks were used to keep students busy and avoid discipline problems.)

2. There was little differentiation among students in their instructional programs. (In the low-achieving schools there was extensive differentiation, with a strong interest in selecting students for compensatory programs.)

3. There were very few so-called write-offs, students perceived as unable to learn and destined to failure. Teachers felt the vast majority were capable of mastering the material. If one teaching strategy did not work, they tried others. (Teachers in the low-achieving schools wrote off large numbers of children as hopeless; many were relegated to remedial classes.)

4. Teachers and principals expressed their belief that students could master the academic work and that they expected them to do so. They were committed to teaching their students to read, do mathematics, and master other academic work. (In the low-achieving schools, teachers and principals believed that stu-

dent ability was low and that grade-level achievement was unrealistic. The teachers took little responsibility for their students' achievement.)

5. Students perceived that they were expected to learn, and they accepted the school academic norms as a standard of high achievement. (In the less successful schools, students perceived that little was expected from them and that achievement norms were low.)

6. Students felt that they had control over their academic work and that the school system was not stacked against them. (Students in the low-achieving schools felt the system functioned so that they could not achieve and that teachers were not committed to high student achievement.)

7. Students believed that what they did could make a difference in their success and that teachers cared about their academic performance. (Students in the ineffective schools experienced feelings of futility about their academic performances and felt that peers would tease them if they tried to achieve.)

8. Teachers consistently rewarded students for demonstrated achievement, a reinforcement pattern that encouraged higher achievement. (Teachers in the low-achieving schools often used confusing or inappropriate reinforcement practices, for example, praising students regardless of the correctness of their responses.)

9. Teaching games involving teams were used. The games reflected high expectations, allowed appropriate reinforcement, and emphasized (cooperative) team learning and attitudes of "try a little harder." (In the low-achieving schools, games were not mentioned or else were not used in ways that stimulated achievement.)

10. The principal was heavily involved in instructional leadership, visiting classrooms often and assuming responsibility for the educational functions of the school. (Principals of the low-achieving mostly white and mostly black schools tended to be disciplinarians and administrators, not strong instructional leaders.)

Note that principal leadership, high expectations, and an academic school climate again surface as critical features of school effectiveness, along with specific favorable teaching and management practices that stimulate academic attitudes and high engagement.

A related project by Brookover and Lezotte (1979) was a case study of eight Michigan elementary schools. Six of the schools were identified by the Michigan Department of Education as showing consistent pupil improvement in basic skills, while two showed a decline. To identify characteristics and patterns related to the rising or falling achievement, the researchers conducted interviews and administered questionnaires to school personnel.

With minor variations, the findings duplicate and supplement what we have seen. In the improving schools,

1. The principal was more of an instructional leader and assumed responsibility for the achievement of basic objectives.

2. Staff members emphasized mastery of basic reading and mathematics objectives. Teachers were committed to and assumed responsibility for teaching these skills.

3. Teachers believed that all students were capable of mastering the basic objectives, and they perceived that the principal shared this belief. Teachers even reported higher (and increasing) levels of student ability.

4. More time was spent in the direct teaching of reading and mathematics.

5. Staff members held decidedly higher (and increasing) achievement expectations of students.

6. Staff accepted the notion of accountability and accepted standardized achievement test results as an indication of effectiveness.

7. Teachers showed more tension and dissatisfaction with existing conditions, compared with the higher satisfaction and morale of teachers in declining schools (which resulted, apparently, from their complacency regarding the school status quo).

8. Staff tended not to place students in compensatory, remedial programs.

Secondary Schools in London

In a unique study, Rutter, Maugham, Mortimore, Ouston, and Smith (1979) invested more than 4 years studying 12 urban secondary schools in London, England. In addition to their focus on secondary schools, another rare feature was their attention to outcomes other than reading and mathematics, namely, attendance, student behavior (late arrival, off-task and disruptive activities), employment, and delinquency, along with the achievement scores. For later comparison, they gathered data on their students at age 10 (verbal reasoning, parent occupation, behavior problems), 4 years before looking at the effects of secondary school characteristics and practices when the same students were 14 years old.

Rutter and his associates first confirmed that (a) effective schools did indeed exist, as reflected in substantially higher achievement levels and fewer behavior problems, and (b) the success of these schools could not be attributed to family economic factors or to students' test scores and behaviors at age 10.

The researchers observed classes for 1 week in each of the 12 schools, coding and recording the activities of the teacher, selected individuals, and the class as a whole. They noted whether the teacher was attending to the subject matter, to students' behavior, to social activities, or to administrative matters. They recorded whether the teacher interacted with individuals or with the entire class. They noted examples of praise or punishment and expressions of warmth or negative feelings. They recorded rates of on-task academic engagement and instances of off-task behavior. On the playground they recorded student activities, misbehavior, and violence and staff reprimands and sanctions.

Before looking at these researchers' often-cited characteristics of effective schools, it is interesting to note that all outcome measures were highly intercorrelated. With few exceptions, schools with the highest academic achievement also showed the highest attendance rates and the fewest behavior problems.

Processes and patterns in these London schools that consistently related to effectiveness included the following:

1. A school-wide academic emphasis and high expectations for academic success. For example, students were treated in ways that emphasized success and their potential for success. Regular homework not only increased academic engagement but symbolized the school's concern for achievement.

2. Staff consensus on the goals and values of the school.

3. A higher proportion of the school week devoted to academic tasks.

4. The establishment of principles and guidelines for student behavior.

5. Classroom management practices that increased students' academic engagement. For example, teachers interacted with the class as a whole rather than individual students, started lessons promptly, minimized interruptions and reprimands, and allowed more frequent periods of independent seatwork.

6. Frequent rewards, praise, and appreciation. Discipline was applied rarely but firmly. (The use of punishment was poorly and inconsistently related to the outcome measures.)

7. Assigning responsibilities for school and personal duties to a large proportion of students, for example, as team captain, homework monitor, or assembly participant. Such assignments improve school attitudes.

8. Providing a clean, comfortable, and pleasant working environment. These comfortable conditions included freedom to use the building during breaks and lunch and access to a telephone.

9. Showing concern for individual students' welfare, for example, as reflected in the feeling among students that they could talk to staff members about personal problems.

In a later thoughtful review of his research, Rutter (1983) concluded that the overall pattern of findings strongly suggested a causative—not just correlational—relationship between school processes and student outcomes. Especially important was the fact that the combined, additive effect of the processes was much stronger than any individual factor. Rutter concluded that the combination of these factors created a *school ethos,* a set of school attitudes, values, and behaviors that fostered achievement and positive behavior.

PORTRAIT OF AN EFFECTIVE SCHOOL

One of the most extensive and thoughtful reviews of research on effective schools was prepared by Purkey and Smith (1983). They analyzed data from four outlier studies, that is, studies that compared highly effective with highly ineffective schools; eight case studies of schools; and six program evaluation studies. The results across the three types of school research projects were remarkably similar, leading Purkey and Smith to propose nine *organizational and structural* variables and four *process* variables contributing to school effectiveness.

Organizational and Structural Variables

Included under organizational and structural variables were many of the leadership, climate, and time-on-task factors that continually surface as hallmarks of effective schooling, along with two items describing relationships with the central district office. Purkey and Smith's specific nine important organizational and structural variables are as follows:

1. School site management. Principals, teachers, and other staff need considerable building-level autonomy to determine how to increase student achievement.

Schools differ in student body composition and groupings and therefore in the particular needs and problems of students. They also differ in community values and expectations; such internal structures as the existing school climate and focus (e.g., athletics or basics), instructional organization, and instructional programs and practices; staff organization and strengths; the goals, values, and expectations of the particular principal and staff; and many other characteristics. In any given school, the unique combination of these factors logically demands flexibility, creativity, and building-level independence—including control of the school budget (Lieberman, 1988; Michaels, 1988)—in order to optimize appropriate improvement plans.

2. Strong instructional leadership by the principal, which is essential to initiate and maintain the school improvement process.

Although individual teachers and groups of teachers certainly can and do work to improve their own effectiveness, as we saw in Chapter 2 the pivotal, causative feature of virtually every effective school is a principal with vision, energy, and a dedication to leading the staff and students toward better school attitudes and higher performance levels. In recent years, this strong leadership increasingly has taken the form of empowering good teachers to observe and help each other improve their teaching techniques (e.g., Haggerson, 1988; Lieberman, 1988; see Chapter 6).

3. Staff stability. Once a school experiences success, keeping its staff together is important for maintaining its effectiveness and promoting further success.

Staff stability naturally contributes to good interpersonal relationships, a good working environment, and shared goals of improving teaching, developing better programs, and generally stimulating an academic climate and higher achievement. Especially disastrous is the selective loss of the best, most effective teachers, perhaps due to frustration over ineffective leadership or the apathetic attitudes of other teachers regarding school improvement.

4. In secondary schools, a planned and purposeful program. This appears to be more beneficial than a program with many electives and few requirements.

In recent years there has been a clear move in the direction of increasing high-school requirements in the basics—mathematics, science, social studies, and English—plus foreign languages. Logically, an increase in requirements implies a decrease in electives, consistent with the Purkey and Smith principle.

5. An effective school-wide staff development program aimed at altering attitudes, expectations, and behavior while teaching teachers new skills and techniques. The training should relate closely to the instructional program.

Regarding the first part of this principle—altering attitudes, expectations, and behavior—Purkey and Smith described school climate (the product of attitudes and expectations) as "a structure, process, and climate of values and norms that channel staff and students in the direction of successful teaching and learning . . . increasing the organizational effectiveness of a school building." As for directly improving the skills of teachers, we saw in Chapter 2 the role of the principal in planning inservice programs that are consistent with the teaching improvement programs. In Chapter 6 we will examine more closely both the observation and supervision roles of the principal as instructional leader and the advantages, benefits, and mechanics of the growing trend toward peer supervision—teachers observing and coaching each other (e.g., Little, 1987).

6. Parent involvement and support and parent awareness of school goals and student responsibilities, especially in regard to homework.

Schools are open systems, that is, systems that interact with the external environment (Ubben & Hughes, 1987). A school is thus more than a set of interrelated internal elements; it affects and is affected by the outside world, especially parents and the community. Parent involvement should extend beyond the occasional parent–teacher conference or open house. Some teachers ask parents to read to their children and listen to their children read; to drill their children on mathematics and spelling; or to help with other homework. Some teachers invite parents to sit in on their classes to see how their children are being taught. Such experience can give parents ideas for teaching children at home (U.S. Department of Education, 1986, 1987; Walberg, 1984). If parents thoroughly understand school expectations regarding homework, whether at the elementary or secondary level, they can help arrange the home environment to accommodate that homework. Many reform plans, the South Carolina state plan (T. Peterson, 1988), for example, include parent involvement.

7. School-wide recognition of academic success; publicly honoring academic achievements.

As we saw in Chapter 2, an effective principal can incorporate many reward mechanisms to recognize achievement, for example, high visibility in the school and in the media for student and staff accomplishments.

8. Maximized learning time, which means devoting a greater proportion of the school day to academic subjects. Students also spend more time during class periods in active learning.

While it is listed as item number 8 by Purkey and Smith, increasing academic engagement is seen as number 1 in importance by many researchers who study effective schools and effective teachers. In Chapter 5 we will examine many steps teachers can take to increase academic engagement, that is, to maximize learning time.

9. District support for fundamental changes and improvements, building-level management, staff stability, and so forth. Guiding and helping, according to Purkey and Smith, is probably the best role for the district office.

Process Variables

The four process variables were described by Purkey and Smith as "the dynamic of the school," responsible for an atmosphere that increases student achievement. These include the following:

1. Collaborative planning and good collegial relationships, both of which are essential for change.

Teachers will not be particularly receptive to changes that are imposed on them from above unless the relationship with the principal and/or department head is good and the changes are planned together. Teacher group planning was listed by Lieberman (1988) as an important component of second-wave educational reform. While concern for good interpersonal and working relationships seems obvious, complaints in the teachers' lounge often focus on policies that were installed without teacher input or collaborative planning and in a less-than-pleasant social atmosphere. In Chapter 6 we will take a longer look at this important aspect of improving teaching—teachers working together in work groups and teaching teams and even observing and coaching each other.

2. A school-wide sense of community and the individual's sense of being a recognizable member of that community. According to Purkey and Smith (1983), it may be created by "the appropriate use of ceremony, symbols, rules (e.g., dress codes), and the like."

A sense of community also may be strengthened by the motivational mechanisms mentioned in Chapter 2, for example, school T-shirts, songs, slogans, and posters and high visibility of school academic and athletic accomplishments. Mechanisms used to create successful corporate cultures—shaping values, establishing heroes to emulate, and using rites and rituals—will be discussed in Chapter 6.

3. Clear goals and high expectations that are commonly shared. These allow the school to direct its resources and functions toward realizing these goals. Clear goals also help reduce student alienation. Continual monitoring of student and class progress is a logical means of determining whether or not goals are being realized. Such monitoring also stimulates and directs staff energy and attention.

Goals may be academic in nature, for example, focusing on increasing learning time, improving teaching and management techniques, or raising achievement levels in basic skill areas. However, looking beyond the basics, school goals can also include teaching thinking skills such as creativity and critical thinking; improving the school climate, student attitudes, and academic motivation; reducing absenteeism, misbehavior, and dropping out; fostering good self-concepts, attitudes, and values; fostering independence; and others.

The school staff may assemble a School Beliefs Statement similar to the one presented in Inset 3-2. Such a formal statement

INSET 3–2

School Beliefs Statement

In order to clarify school goals and help establish a proper climate and direction, Ubben and Hughes (1987) recommended that formal *belief statements* be prepared. These are best created by writing teams whose members include teachers of various grades and subjects and perhaps a community member and a secondary student. The teams create one or more belief statements for each topic, for example, the role of the principal, the role of teachers, the curriculum, academic achievement, recognizing student individuality, student affective and social development, global school goals, and so forth. To create the final document, representatives from each team form a consensus team, which ratifies, modifies, and combines the belief statements into a final comprehensive and cohesive "We believe" statement. An example follows.

> *We believe that Lincoln High School is a unique educational environment. Its uniqueness is exemplified in certain aspects of its design. It is designed to meet the individual needs of a larger percentage of students than is possible in the traditional system; to avoid a mass-produced, molding effect; to provide a distinctly pleasant atmosphere for learning; to foster respectful relationships; and to serve the community.*
>
> *We believe that all students are unique as individuals—that they develop at different rates and in different manners. We believe that all students have needs that must be fulfilled. We believe that students have a natural desire to learn independence, responsibility, self-assertion, democratic ideas, and the skills necessary to solve present and future problems.*
>
> *We believe that the role of the student is to involve himself or herself responsibly in the learning experience.*

Adapted with permission from *The Principal: Creative Leadership for Effective Schools*, by Gerald C. Ubben and Larry W. Hughes (Allyn and Bacon, 1987), pp. 95, 97–99.

(continued)

We believe that learning is evidenced by a behavioral change. It is a continuous process that takes place in the home, community, and school.

We believe that the role of the teacher is (a) to design learning opportunities and (b) to provide each student for whom the teacher is responsible the freedom to learn what he or she needs to take a productive and rewarding part in society. The teacher is an advisor and sharer.

We believe that teaching and learning can best be accomplished through interaction and involvement of students, staff, administration, and community.

We believe that the administration is responsible for supplying and maintaining all of the physical accoutrements of the school. The principal is to be an instructional leader, but shares with students, teachers, and community the task of facilitating and coordinating learning. The principal's leadership should be participatory and not authoritarian.

We believe that the purpose of Lincoln High School is to establish a student and community learning center with high expectations for student performance designed to facilitate stimulating learning experiences and harmonious social interactions in which each individual has the opportunity to realize his or her full potential.

It is our endeavor to develop the following qualities to a high degree through conscientious and dedicated guidance and instruction. These qualities are

1. *The self-evaluative ability of each individual.*
2. *Positive attitudes of individuals toward themselves and others.*
3. *Independence and responsibility in the individual.*
4. *Creativity in the individual.*
5. *The ability to be self-assertive.*
6. *The acquiring of knowledge relative to both the mental and physical needs and abilities of the individual.*
7. *The critical thinking and decision-making ability of the individual.*
8. *The ability of the individual to contribute to and make his or her way in our society.*

helps raise the awareness of staff and students of the goals and purposes of the school in a concrete way.

4. Better classroom control, order, and discipline, which reflect the seriousness and purpose with which the school approaches its task. Rules should be clear, reasonable, and fairly and consistently enforced. Such procedures not only reduce behavior problems but promote feelings of pride and responsibility. Classroom management will be explored briefly later in this chapter and more fully in Chapter 4.

Purkey and Smith concluded that these organizational—structural and process variables can create a new school climate that will develop over time as leadership, staff, and students begin thinking and behaving in new ways. The Purkey and Smith integration incorporates core principles of effective schooling that have appeared in previous sections and chapters, and will be emphasized in later chapters on classroom management, effective teaching, and classroom observation and supervision. Most of the principles remain part of second-wave educational reform (e.g., Lieberman, 1988; Michaels, 1988; see Chapter 6).

ADDITIONAL CHARACTERISTICS OF EFFECTIVE SCHOOLS

In addition to the findings of Weber (1971), Edmonds (1979), Brookover and his colleagues (1979, 1982), and Rutter (1983) and the integrated portrait by Purkey and Smith (1983), there are other characteristics of effective schools that have surfaced in study after study in recent years (e.g., Austin & Garber, 1985; Blumberg & Greenfield, 1986; Lipsitz, 1983; T. Peterson, 1988; Sergiovanni, 1987; Squires, Huitt, & Segars, 1983; Ubben & Hughes, 1987; U.S. Department of Education, 1986, 1987). The five main categories of specific characteristics of effective schools discussed here include (1) good classroom management practices, (2) high academic engagement, (3) monitoring of student progress, (4) instructional improvement as a school priority, and (5) clear goals and objectives. Most of these also will appear in Chapter 5 under the heading of "Effective Teachers," but the emphasis here is on the school-wide perspective.

GOOD CLASSROOM
MANAGEMENT PRACTICES

A consistent characteristic of effective schools is that teachers maintain a good balance between their classroom management skills and their instructional skills (e.g, New York State Department of Education, 1974). As for specific management techniques, Kounin's (1977) principles of good classroom management (Chapter 4) have been confirmed again and again.

As a brief overview, high achievement is associated with *withitness* on the part of the teacher—being aware of what is going on and making sure that the students know the teacher is aware. The teacher must also be accurate in the target and timing of reprimands; that is, the right person must be reprimanded, and promptly. The target and timing of praise also is important.

Another of Kounin's main principles that has been confirmed repeatedly is that smooth, rapid, and disruption-free transitions between activities are related to reduced deviancy and higher achievement. Also, variety in activities, media, location, and level of thinking sustains motivation and interest and reduces satiation and boredom.

Another good management principle is to start class quickly and purposefully, with assignments and activities set to go and supplies and materials ready. Such an approach not only avoids wasting time but emphasizes the academic purpose of the class. Handling routine administrative matters quickly and efficiently also minimizes disruptions and increases learning time.

The academic climate of the classroom may be further enhanced by maintaining an orderly and pleasant, yet businesslike classroom atmosphere that emphasizes purpose and is conducive to learning.

Orderliness is aided by having a written code, understood by staff, students, and parents, that specifies both high standards for acceptable behavior and the disciplinary consequences of student misbehavior. Rules are taught and reviewed from the beginning of the year or semester.

If needed, disciplinary action is administered quickly, in a manner consistent with the rules, and equitably for all students. Discipline is neutral, matter of fact, and focused on the poor behavior, not the person. With such an approach, fair play will come to be expected. Humiliation of students is to be avoided, as is the modeling of violence.

Generally, according to Cohen (1983), managing students is easier if a school can establish a moral order that includes respect for authority, genuine caring about individuals, respect for their feelings and attitudes, mutual trust, and the consistent enforcement of norms that define and delimit acceptable behavior. Much more will be said about this subject in Chapter 4.

HIGH ACADEMIC ENGAGEMENT

Another consistent and central feature of effective schools is that their students spend more time actively engaged in learning. While this principle is virtually common sense, it continues to receive high-level attention as a core goal for improving student achievement (e.g., Purkey & Smith, 1983; Ubben & Hughes, 1987; U.S. Department of Education, 1986, 1987). As much as is reasonably possible, school time is used for learning, and time spent on noninstructional activities and unassigned time is minimized.

The school calendar and school events can be scheduled to minimize the loss of classroom learning time. Administrators and teachers should ask questions such as the following:

> Are holidays, spring breaks, parent–teacher conferences, and state teacher conferences planned so that the number of class days set by the state education department is maintained?

> Must fire or earthquake drills or school assemblies break up the best morning hours for concentration?

> Is it necessary for school athletes to miss 1 or 2 class hours to suit up for a game?

> Should theater rehearsals replace class time?

The practice of pulling students out of regular classes for nonacademic activities should be monitored and minimized.

Academic engagement is aided when classes and other activities start and end on time. Effective teachers set and maintain a brisk pace that is consistent with thorough learning. Time-use guidelines and time allocations (priorities) among subjects should be established and followed, with the teacher using clear start and stop cues to help pace lessons within the time guidelines.

Some schools and teachers, particularly those with a mastery orientation, have adopted the policy that if students do not finish their work during class extra learning time is found. For example, students may work on lessons during lunch or before or after school in order to maintain high levels of mastery.

MONITORING STUDENT PROGRESS

If a school staff is serious about increasing student achievement, that achievement must be closely monitored via test results, grade reports, attendance records, and other methods, and changes must be made in school procedures and instructional programs to meet identified needs and weaknesses. Such monitoring may include the following practices:

- Holding students accountable for their work.

- Monitoring student learning via informal observation and contact.

- Developing and using simple and efficient routines for collecting, summarizing, and reporting achievement data related to learning objectives.

- Establishing and periodically updating individual students' records and group summaries. Both individual data and scores for classes and grades are reviewed over time to detect changing trends.

- Using assessment results to evaluate the effectiveness of teaching methods.

- Encouraging parents to monitor student progress.

INSTRUCTIONAL IMPROVEMENT AS A SCHOOL PRIORITY

As we have seen, a high staff dedication to improving the instructional program is intimately tied to an academic climate, the expectation that all students can learn, and leadership practices aimed at improving teaching methods and instructional programs. Strong staff goals of instructional improvement have been consistently related to school effectiveness (Edmonds, 1979; Gage & Berliner, 1984; Greenfield, 1987; T. Peterson, 1988; Purkey & Smith, 1983).

This dedication to instructional improvement includes setting goals and priorities for improving student performance that are in accord with district guidelines, community goals, and building-level conceptions of what a good school is. Instructional improvement logically includes organizing specific and systematic improvement strategies designed to reach these goals. For teachers to feel commitment to instructional improvements, they must be empowered to plan them and carry them out. The plans are given high priority and visibility, and their implementation is carefully monitored by teachers and administrators. Support and participation by teachers are also monitored; commitments must be made and consistently followed through. Teachers are expected to meet high instructional standards.

Everyone, from the district superintendent to the smallest student, should accept the notion that school exists as a place for learning.

CLEAR GOALS AND OBJECTIVES

Having clear goals and objectives is intimately linked to all of the other features of effective schools. Good management practices, high task engagement, monitoring of progress, instructional leadership, expectations of success, and instructional improvement as a high priority all combine in an effort to reach reasonable goals and objectives.

Note that there are clear and obvious relationships among learning goals (where you want to go), instructional activities (how to get there), and evaluations of student learning (how to know you have arrived).

Setting clear goals and objectives normally includes developing and prioritizing them according to district and building-level guidelines. Teachers review, select, and approve the objectives and organize them into units or lessons according to a timeline. They also match instructional resources and teaching activities to the objectives and record this information in lesson plans. Alternative resources and activities also are planned. After the lessons have been taught, teachers review and modify the resources and activities in order to increase their effectiveness.

ASSESSING SCHOOL EXCELLENCE

Ubben and Hughes (1987) have recommended that the administration and staff of any school concerned with improving effectiveness create a School Excellence Inventory. Such an inventory serves as a needs assessment device. That is, it is designed to evaluate the achievement of stated school goals and beliefs and identify areas that need improvement. Topics for evaluation can include those specifically described in the school's belief statement (Inset 3-2). In fact, Ubben and Hughes suggested that the belief statement be used as a guide for creating items for a tailor-made school excellence inventory.

Figure 3-1 presents a sample school excellence inventory that evaluates perceptions of success in the areas of (1) on-task engagement, (2) school climate, (3) commitment to an academic focus, (4) staff expectations and performance, (5) curriculum, (6) leadership effectiveness, and (7) the evaluation and monitoring of student progress. A similar device can be designed to fit any school's goals and priorities by writing a half dozen items that clearly focus on each goal, belief, or dimension of effectiveness. Such inventories should always include a space for written comments that will enrich the information gained from the inventory.

The inventory is filled out by all school administrators, faculty, and staff, as well as other persons who are knowledgeable about the school, for example, teacher aides, volunteers, and parents. Allowing critics of the school to fill in the questionnaire can illuminate weaknesses or misconceptions about school goals and programs.

The sample scoring guide in Figure 3-1 illustrates how each topic area, belief, or dimension of effectiveness is objectively scored.

COMMENTARY

In Chapter 1 under the heading "Is the Effective-Schools Movement a Passing Fad?" we noted that some pessimistic educators have considered the effective-schooling movement to be the

FIGURE 3–1
School Excellence Inventory

Directions: Please rate the following items on a scale of 1 to 5 to reflect your opinion of your school (1 = low, 3 = neutral, 5 = high).

		low	*high*

1. Students have favorable attitudes toward school and learning.   1 2 3 4 5

2. Student learning is evaluated using measures closely related to the curriculum content.   1 2 3 4 5

3. The staff has high expectations for the students and adults with whom they work.   1 2 3 4 5

4. Student time-on-task behavior is maintained at a high level because
   (a) A climate of order and discipline has been established.   1 2 3 4 5
   (b) Little time is used for maintaining order.   1 2 3 4 5
   (c) Good classroom management practices maximize available instructional time.   1 2 3 4 5
   (d) The school staff has made a commitment to maximize available learning time by reducing impediments to learning and interruptions of the school day.   1 2 3 4 5

5. Students and parents receive regular feedback regarding each student's progress.   1 2 3 4 5

6. Student attendance rates are high.   1 2 3 4 5

7. There is a clear understanding of what the school believes in and stands for, which includes
   (a) An academic focus.   1 2 3 4 5
   (b) A belief that all students have the ability to learn.   1 2 3 4 5
   (c) An expectation that each student will learn.   1 2 3 4 5
   (d) High expectations for each student.   1 2 3 4 5

Adapted with permission from *The Principal: Creative Leadership for Effective Schools*, by Gerald C. Ubben and Larry W. Hughes (Allyn and Bacon, 1987), pp. 95, 97–99.

(continued)

		low	high

8. Teachers regularly employ techniques to assure that all students are learning.   1 2 3 4 5

9. Staff members are evaluated regularly.   1 2 3 4 5

10. Programs and varied instructional techniques are provided in order to respond to each child's individual needs and differences.   1 2 3 4 5

11. Students feel valued and successful.   1 2 3 4 5

12. Individual help is provided to students when needed.   1 2 3 4 5

13. Members of the school staff exhibit a high degree of concern and commitment for the achievement and well-being of each student.   1 2 3 4 5

14. The principal is effective because he or she
    (a) Understands the process of instruction and accepts responsibility for being an instructional leader.   1 2 3 4 5
    (b) Is an able manager.   1 2 3 4 5
    (c) Has high, attainable expectations for the students and adults with whom he or she works.   1 2 3 4 5
    (d) Has clear goals (a clear sense of purpose and priorities) and is able to enlist the support of others in understanding, accepting, and accomplishing those ends.   1 2 3 4 5
    (e) Recognizes the importance of (and actively involves) the people who work in and are served by the school.   1 2 3 4 5
    (f) Assists the school staff in implementing sound instructional practices.   1 2 3 4 5

15. Students receive prompt feedback on specific assignments.   1 2 3 4 5

16. Staff and student morale is high.   1 2 3 4 5

17. Members of the school staff cooperate with and support each other.   1 2 3 4 5

18. The curriculum
    (a) Emphasizes mastery of basic skills.   1 2 3 4 5
    (b) Is well defined.   1 2 3 4 5
    (c) Is appropriately sequenced and articulated from grade to grade and from subject to subject.   1 2 3 4 5

	low high
(d) Includes clearly defined learner goals.	1 2 3 4 5
(e) Is evaluated regularly.	1 2 3 4 5

19. Techniques are used to pinpoint individual students' strengths and weaknesses.   1 2 3 4 5

20. The staff is competent and continues to grow and learn.   1 2 3 4 5

21. The school is open to and encourages participation and involvement by parents and other citizens.   1 2 3 4 5

22. Parents, students, and staff place a high priority on learning.   1 2 3 4 5

23. Students are instructed at the appropriate level of difficulty.   1 2 3 4 5

Summary Sheet
School Excellence Inventory

Time	Climate	Basic Commitment	Staff	Curriculum	Leadership	Evaluation
#4a = ___	#1 = ___	#7a = ___	#3 = ___	#10 = ___	#14a = ___	#2 = ___
#4b = ___	#6 = ___	#7b = ___	#9 = ___	#18a = ___	#14b = ___	#5 = ___
#4c = ___	#11 = ___	#7c = ___	#13 = ___	#18b = ___	#14c = ___	#8 = ___
#4d = ___	#16 = ___	#7d = ___	#17 = ___	#18c = ___	#14d = ___	#12 = ___
Total = ___	#21 = ___	#22 = ___	#20 = ___	#18d = ___	#14e = ___	#15 = ___
÷4 = ___	Total = ___	Total = ___	Total = ___	#18e = ___	#14f = ___	#19 = ___
	÷5 = ___	÷5 = ___	÷5 = ___	Total = ___	Total = ___	#23 = ___
				÷6 = ___	÷6 = ___	Total = ___
						÷7 = ___

---

teaching machines and new math of the 1980s—a fad that will disappear when another educational fashion catches the fancy of educators and the public. Reform critic Cuban (1988), for example, stated that "we are plagued by optimism and 'ought to be's' and 'shoulds' of educational reformers." He argued in favor of stability rather than change. Mackenzie (1983), however, has reflected our own attitudes in arguing the case for the validity of principles of effective schooling and for the notion that schools should change in the direction of those principles. There are solid and logical reasons why the effective-schooling movement is no passing fad.

First, as Mackenzie emphasized, the school improvement recommendations stemming from effective schooling studies are "deeply rooted in common sense . . . and appeal directly to . . . the daily experience of working educators." There have been almost "audible gasps of relief by reviewer after reviewer, that active and committed educational leaders can indeed do something about the conditions for achievement in the nation's schools" (Mackenzie, 1983).

The intuitive appeal of its core principles has led some educational researchers, for example, Edmonds (1981, 1982) and perhaps Brookover and Lezotte (Brookover et al., 1982), to become activist advocates of effective schooling.

Also, as Mackenzie noted, much of the research has grown directly from the concerns of state and district boards of education (e.g., Minneapolis Board of Education, 1981; New York State Department of Education, 1974), and the results have been rapidly and successfully translated into action for school improvement at the state and district level. The description of "positive learning climates" published by the Minneapolis Board of Education (1981) might have been lifted directly from reviews of research on effective schools and teaching.

Still another reason for the logical appeal and soundness of the effective-school principles stems from the convergent nature of the research. Indeed, the many forms of research—at elementary and secondary levels, in rich and poor communities, and in more than one country—are impressive in that they identify many of the same core principles. As Mackenzie noted, principles derived from case studies of effective schools are supported by evidence from descriptive studies, correlational research, experimental studies, and evaluation research, all of which have been conducted on effective schools, principals, and teachers. Many of these principles are "being digested into strategic recommendations for school improvement" (Mackenzie, 1983). We noted earlier that the widely disseminated U.S. Department of Education (1986, 1987) document, *What Works: Research About Teaching and Learning,* directly reflects Weber's and Edmonds's recommendations as presented in this chapter.

The principles and the school improvement programs based on them do not offer a quick solution. Indeed, as we have seen, perhaps 5 years are needed for a well-planned program to become successful. T. Peterson (1988) suggested 3 to 10 years as a reasonable period for educational reforms to be successfully implemented.

It is also worth mentioning that the so-called second-wave educational reform movement, reviewed briefly in Chapter 6, retains virtually all of the core characteristics revealed by research on effective schools, principals, and teachers. There is, however, a greater emphasis on empowering teachers to be responsible for their own professional improvement rather than the paternalistic approach of depending on the principal to direct school and teaching improvement. For example, peer observation and coaching are more strongly recommended, an emphasis leading to the development of teacher centers where excellent teachers can work on release time to improve the teaching skills and techniques of other teachers.

Finally, Austin and Holowenzak (1985) have described the following certain way to recognize a successful, effective school:

> *We think that one of the best criteria that you might use to judge an exceptional school in your county would be to ask the principal of the school to show you the waiting list they have of people who want to teach at their school. Just as teachers know intuitively who are the really great teachers in their schools, they also know the best schools in the district. Exceptional schools have waiting lists of people who want to transfer into them.*

SUMMARY

The topics of effective schools, effective principals, and effective teachers are intermixed and based on much the same research literature. Three elementary assumptions are that unusually effective schools can be identified; they exhibit recurrent characteristics that educators can manipulate; and the characteristics provide a basis for improving unsuccessful schools.

Purkey and Smith suggested that effective and ineffective schools should not be compared with each other, but with average schools.

SES level must be controlled in research or identified school differences will be meaningless. For example, identifying characteristics of low-SES effective schools may not help in improving middle-class schools.

Most effective-schooling research has taken place in elementary schools, which differ in many ways from secondary schools. Moreover, the research has usually involved just one or two grades, not the entire school.

With observational and correlational research, causal ordering may be ambiguous; for example, high achievement may cause the high expectations rather than the reverse.

Critics have charged that describing effective schools is not the same as creating effective schools. However, researchers have successfully trained principals and teachers, resulting in raised achievement scores. Conclusions regarding average school achievement may not apply to various ethnic or SES groups within the school.

Some portion of the differences found between effective and ineffective schools is due to random error. Although it has been estimated that only about 4.5% of the differences in individual student achievement are due to differences between schools, that percentage is important.

There is no single combination of variables that will work to raise the effectiveness of every school.

In response to the Coleman Report, Weber studied four inner-city schools that were effective in teaching reading. These schools showed strong instructional leadership, high achievement expectations, an academic atmosphere, a strong emphasis on reading, frequent evaluations of progress, a high concern for the progress of each student, and additional reading personnel. Class size, achievement grouping, and the quality of the physical building were not important.

Edmonds's classic list of characteristics of effective schools is similar to that of Weber: strong instructional leadership; high expectations; an academic atmosphere; a focus on basic skills; focusing energy and resources on these fundamental objectives; and frequent monitoring of progress. Milwaukee's Project Rise and the New York City School Improvement Project were based on Edmonds's principles.

The research of Brookover, Lezotte, and their colleagues showed that effective schools allocated most of the school day to instruction (not just keeping students busy); most students participated in the same program (were not put into compensatory programs); teacher expectations for achievement were high; there were few so-called write-offs; students perceived they were expected to achieve; teachers rewarded students for demonstrated achievement; the principal was heavily involved in instruction; and teaching games allowed appropriate reinforcement, cooperative learning, and attitudes of "try harder."

Brookover and Lezotte's research duplicated and overlapped earlier studies, emphasizing instructional leadership by the principal; a commitment to teaching basic skills; a strong belief that all students can master basic skills; high achievement expectations; more time spent directly teaching reading and mathematics; acceptance of standardized test results as evidence of effectiveness; and not placing students in compensatory programs.

Rutter's London study with secondary students confirmed that effective schools existed and that effectiveness could not be attributed to family economic factors or to students' scores and behaviors at age 10. The following factors were important to effectiveness: an academic emphasis; high expectations; staff consensus on school goals; student behavior guidelines; good classroom management that increased engagement; frequent rewards and praise; assigning duties and responsibilities to many students; a pleasant environment; and showing concern for individual students' welfare.

Purkey and Smith's portrait of an effective school identified nine organizational and structural variables: school site autonomy; strong leadership; staff stability; planned and purposeful secondary programs; school-wide staff development; parent involvement and support; school-wide and public recognition of academic success; and maximized learning time. They identified four process variables: collaborative planning and good collegial relationships; a school-wide sense of community; clear goals and high expectations; and improved classroom control and discipline.

Additional characteristics that contribute to school effectiveness fell into the categories of good classroom management, high academic engagement, monitoring student progress, instructional improvement as a school priority, and clear goals and objectives.

A school excellence inventory can serve as a needs assessment instrument, evaluating such topics as degree of academic engagement, school climate and academic focus, staff expectations and performance, curriculum, leadership, and monitoring progress.

The intuitive appeal of the major principles of school effectiveness and the broad base of research support strongly suggest that the movement is not a temporary fad.

Chapter Four

Classroom Management

*Good discipline requires managing the classroom so
that opportunities for disruption are minimized and so
that it is easy for students to engage in learning
activities. . . . The key to good discipline is preventing
inappropriate behavior in the first place, and when it
occurs dealing with it promptly and relatively
unobtrusively before it escalates or intensifies.*
—Edmund T. Emmer, "Classroom Management and Discipline"

The importance of good classroom management cannot be over-
stated. We noted in Chapter 1 that successful teaching and classroom management are inseparable. Experts have said that management is a part of instruction (Jones & Jones, 1986; Sanford,
Emmer, & Clements, 1983) or a prerequisite for instruction
(Doyle, 1985). Either way, there is a close relationship between
good management and good achievement, behavior, and attitudes.

Management skills and techniques are especially critical for
beginning teachers, since an inability to maintain order will hardly
promote businesslike engagement and good achievement. Further, teachers' ability to control students will weigh heavily in their
evaluations and ratings. More than one idealistic young teacher
has been driven from the classroom by continual problems with
students.

Emmer (1987) defined classroom management as "a set of
teacher behaviors and activities directed at engaging students in
appropriate behavior and minimizing disruptions." Another man-

The authors are indebted to Bonnie L. Williams for her contributions to this chapter.

agement expert, Duke (1979), said classroom management is "the provisions and procedures necessary to establish and maintain an environment in which instruction and learning can occur." Both definitions directly imply that good management is largely preventative. That is, the teacher takes *advance* action to prevent inattention, off-task behavior, or disruptiveness. Some describe the preventative approach as *good* discipline, which contrasts sharply with the usual interpretation of discipline as punishing misbehavior after it occurs. The latter is the usual response of teachers.

Good discipline is a broad concept, encompassing an academic classroom climate and effective teaching practices, both of which promote the high engagement and good attitudes that intrinsically prevent misbehavior. Good discipline also includes placing limits on students and reducing opportunities for inappropriate behavior.

It is not easy to achieve good discipline. It is complicated, for example, by the necessity for group teaching, which regularly produces confusion for some students and boredom for others. Seatwork and other assignments vary in interest value for different students, and students sometimes do not know what they are supposed to do when they finish their work and the teacher is busy with others. Denscombe (1985) noted that students are not passive; their actions and reactions are often unpredictable. Clowning, talking, poking, and sailing airplanes are common ways for students to release tension; after all, they cannot take a coffee break when they get restless.

Peer approval of clowning or defiance is another cause of misbehavior. There also are such deep-rooted and troublesome causes of disruptiveness as poverty and alienation, parental rejection, frustration due to low ability, irrelevant curriculum, crowded and impersonal schools, emotional or adjustment problems, poor self-image, and peer traditions of rebellion and defiance.

The following is a preview of frequent classroom management or good-discipline recommendations, many of which will be elaborated in this chapter. In the category of *rules and expectations,* teachers concerned with good management will

- Establish positive expectations and a good working relationship, creating an orderly, pleasant, businesslike atmosphere.

- In accord with the *withitness* principle, let students know that the teacher knows what is going on.

- Establish clear and reasonable rules, but as few as possible. The rules specify standards for acceptable behavior and the consequences of misbehavior. The rules are taught and reviewed from the beginning of the year.
- Let students know they are accountable for their behavior and their assignments.

There also are *classroom organizational* steps to take. Teachers can

- Arrange the room for continual teacher surveillance.
- Plan for smooth and efficient transitions between activities.
- Plan for interest, using variety in activities, content, level of thinking, media, and location to reduce satiation and boredom.
- Remove stimuli—equipment, materials, or friends—that set off clowning, talking, and other forms of inappropriate behavior.

In terms of *classroom activities,* teachers can

- Start class quickly and purposefully, with materials, assignments, and activities planned, organized, and ready to go.
- Keep students engaged in learning or other activities.
- Be sure students know what to do when they finish their seatwork.

In *response to misbehavior or deviancy,* good classroom managers will

- Ignore minor undesirable behavior, instead of reinforcing it with attention.
- Use humor or threats before using punishment.
- If needed, administer discipline quickly, in a manner that is consistent with the rules and fair for all students. Discipline is neutral, matter of fact, and focused on the behavior, not the person. Humiliation of students is avoided, as is the modeling of violence.

STRATEGIES FOR PREVENTING AND STOPPING MISBEHAVIOR

One of the most thorough research efforts aimed at identifying principles and techniques of effective classroom management was a 5-year research project by Jacob Kounin (1970). Kounin's principles have been confirmed repeatedly in recent studies of characteristics of effective teachers and well-managed classrooms (e.g., Brophy & Evertson, 1976; Copeland, 1983; Emmer & Evertson, 1981; Emmer, Evertson, & Anderson, 1980; Evertson & Emmer, 1982; see also Doyle, 1985; Emmer, 1987).

Withitness and Overlapping

Kounin's premier trait of good management was dubbed *withitness*—the ability to communicate to students that the teacher knows what is going on in the classroom. According to Kounin, it is not good enough to just announce, "I know what's going on." Teachers must demonstrate by actual behavior that they have "eyes in the back of their heads." Kounin measured withitness by videotaping classes in progress, focusing on how accurately teachers correct misbehaving students. Teachers were given a low withitness score if the *target* of a request to desist was the wrong student, or if the *timing* of the request was incorrect. For example: Lucy and John are whispering and then Robert joins in. Jane starts to giggle and says something to John. Mary leans over and whispers to Jane. Finally Ms. Smith, who scores low in withitness, says, "Mary and Jane, please stop that!" In this case, both the target and the timing are wrong, and the message to students is that Ms. Smith does not know what is going on. A teacher with a high withitness score would identify and censure the correct targets, Lucy and John, before the deviancy spreads to other students.

Mistakes in targeting include asking the wrong child (e.g., a later participant or an onlooker rather than the initiator) to desist or putting an end to a less serious deviancy while overlooking a more serious one. Timing mistakes amount to being late with the request to desist, for example, allowing deviancy to spread among class members or to take a more serious form (e.g., talking becoming shoving) before it is dealt with.

Brooks (1985) and Evertson and Emmer (1982) recommended that teachers communicate their awareness or withitness by visually scanning the group and making eye contact with students engaged in inappropriate behavior. Emmer, Evertson, and Anderson (1980) noted that effective classroom managers do not appear to treat inappropriate behavior differently than ineffective managers—they just do it sooner.

Overlapping is another of Kounin's principles of effective classroom management. Basically, overlapping is the handling of two classroom matters at once, especially attending to deviancy without disrupting an ongoing learning activity. A teacher who does not overlap will become immersed in one matter only and neglect the other. For example, imagine that Mr. Georgia is working with a microcomputer group when across the room Grant and Lee begin sword-fighting with rulers. The nonoverlapping Mr. Georgia promptly stops the computer group and asks Grant and Lee to reach a truce and return to their seatwork. A more effective, overlapping teacher might say, "Jan, you show the group how a GOTO statement works" and then turn to squelch Grant and Lee.

Other instances of overlapping might involve two instructional activities. For example, a teacher might be supervising small-group mathematics work when a student walks up to ask about a new vocabulary word. If the teacher handles both tasks at once, instead of neglecting one to attend to the other, that is overlapping. The purpose of overlapping is to prevent deviancy or other interruptions from interfering with the learning activity.

Are withitness and overlapping truly important for effective management? Kounin obtained scores on deviancy rates and ratings of task involvement. Sure enough, 49 first- and second-grade classroom teachers who were high in withitness and overlapping also produced higher task involvement and lower deviancy rates in both recitation and seatwork among their students. Withitness and overlapping were highly related, in that teachers with "eyes in the back of their heads" (withitness) also were better able to deal with two matters at once (overlapping).

Monitoring and Prompt Handling

Management expert Emmer (1987) has suggested that Kounin's withitness should be viewed as a combination of two related teaching skills, close monitoring of the class and prompt handling of inappropriate behavior. That is, teachers who are "with it" will be alert to students whose behavior is straying from accepted norms and will promptly stop the inappropriate behavior and redirect students to suitable activities.

Good monitoring involves scanning the room to see what students are doing, keeping track of individual progress, and generally being vigilant regarding student engagement in learning activities. Without close monitoring there is an increased chance that inappropriate behaviors will spread to other students or escalate into more serious problems before the teacher becomes aware of them. As Emmer said, it is easier to deal with mild forms of misbehavior that involve just one or a few students. Furthermore, if misbehavior is permitted to spread it becomes a poor model for other students.

Of course, monitoring by itself is not enough. Monitoring must be complemented by the prompt handling of misbehavior. However, it is neither necessary nor reasonable to respond to *all* instances of inappropriate behavior. According to Emmer, overreacting is as bad as underreacting. It is necessary to deal with instances of misbehavior that are likely to become more intense or spread. In particular, interfering with other students' work, disrupting activities, not following correct procedures or work requirements, and aggressive behavior (playful or not) must be stopped or corrected. Minor violations that might safely be ignored include behaviors that do not interfere with others, are of short duration, or are inadvertent and probably self-correcting, such as violating a hand-raising rule.

Related to Kounin's principle of overlapping, Emmer (1987) recommended handling deviancy in an unobtrusive manner, that is, without stopping a lesson, unnecessarily disrupting other students, or calling undue attention to the deviancy. Most requests to desist, therefore, should be brief and undramatic and should not slow down the current classroom activity. Such low-key interventions would be appropriate for routine misbehaviors such as inattention, wandering, talking too loud, or inappropriate social conversations. However, ongoing activities may reasonably be interrupted to deal with a serious or highly disruptive event such as physical aggression, intimidation, abusive language, or the flagrant violation of important rules.

Four low-key tactics that should not disrupt the lesson or greatly distract other students include the following:

1. Making eye contact with the perpetrator, holding it until the misbehavior stops.

2. Moving closer to the misbehaving student.

3. Using nonverbal signals, particularly a finger to the lips.

4. Stating the student's name, perhaps accompanying it with a brief request to end the misbehavior (Emmer, 1987).

A theoretically important strategy in the category of prompt handling is *redirecting* students from inappropriate to appropriate behavior. It is a positive approach that indicates what the student should do rather than a negative approach of punishing inappropriate behavior. Telling students to stop doing something does not automatically tell them what they *should* be doing. Redirecting an individual student can take several specific forms: reminding the student what behavior is appropriate; asking whether the student knows what he or she is supposed to be doing; or asking the student to state the rule or procedure being violated.

At a group level the teacher can redirect behavior with instructions requiring an overt response that replaces the deviant behavior or that supplies models for appropriate behavior. Emmer (1987) recommended using *many* of the following types of statements rather than overusing any one:

"Let me see everyone's eyes, please."

"Everyone look at the chart on page 24."

"Please write the material on the overhead in your notebooks."

"Everyone look at the chalkboard. What is the next step?"

"I see two tables where students have done a good job cleaning up."

"Most of you are listening and paying attention very well."

"I count ten people who are quiet and have their workbooks out . . . Now I see five more . . . Good."

"Let's wait until everyone is listening."

"I like the way most of you are working together quietly and sharing the materials without arguing."

Kounin's withitness and overlapping and Emmer's extension of them in terms of monitoring and prompt handling of inappropriate behavior—including redirecting—should be high on every teacher's list of preventative (and corrective) classroom management skills.

Smoothness and Momentum

Teachers change learning activities frequently. Sometimes the change is *physical,* as when students move from their seats to a reading circle; sometimes it is *psychological,* as when they switch from a spelling quiz to mathematics. Transitions can be *minor,* as between speaking turns, or *major,* as when changing activities, lessons, or classes (Doyle, 1985). Teachers must signal the onset of a change, reorient the focus, and initiate the new segment. The transition can be smooth and efficient or it can be slow and awkward, providing plenty of opportunity for inattention, distraction, rowdiness, or other inappropriate behavior. According to Doyle (1985), Burns (1984), and Gump (1982), teachers oversee approximately 31 major transitions per day, spending about 15% of class time in the transitions. Transition time includes such housekeeping activities as turning in papers, sharpening pencils, disposing of trash, or getting a drink of water.

Kounin (1970) defined *momentum* as "the absence of slowdowns," that is, keeping the class moving on academic activities. A related concept is *smoothness,* which is the absence of teacher behaviors that disrupt transitions between activities or break up the continuity of an ongoing lesson. In Kounin's words, smoothness is the absence of "behaviors that produce jerky movement." While Kounin measured momentum and smoothness independently, he did find that they were highly intercorrelated (correlation coefficient = .75). Because of their obvious conceptual similarity and the high statistical correlation, most writers just speak of maintaining smoothness and momentum as a valuable managerial skill.

Kounin identified five bad habits that disrupt smoothness and momentum: flip-flops, fragmentation, dangles, stimulus-boundedness, thrusts, and overdwelling.

Flip-flops. With *flip-flops,* a teacher ends one activity (e.g., spelling), begins a second activity (e.g., mathematics), then flops back to the first activity ("How many spelled all of the words correctly?").

Fragmentation. Fragmentation is unnecessarily breaking up an activity into subparts—jerky steps—when it should be performed as a single unit. *Group fragmentation* involves having students do something singly and separately instead of as a unit and at one time. For example, students might be asked to join a reading group one at a time: "Mary, you come and take this seat. Fine. Now Fred, you come and sit there. Good. Janet, now you stand up and come over here," and so on.

Prop fragmentation involves breaking up into unnecessary subparts a meaningful unit of behavior that could have been performed as a single, uninterrupted sequence: "All right everybody, close your spelling books. (Pause) Put away your red pencils. (Pause) Put your spelling books in your desks. (Pause) Take out your arithmetic books and put them on your desks in front of you. (Pause) Let's keep everything off your desks except your arithmetic book. (Pause) Let's sit up straight. (Pause) Now get out your black pencils. (Pause) Now open your book to page 17."

Dangles. With *dangles*, the teacher starts the class on one activity and then suddenly reacts to a different matter, leaving the class dangling. For example, Ms. Kantwate might ask Jean to stand up and read a paragraph and then say, "My goodness, Richard isn't here today. Does anyone know if Richard is ill?" Jean and the rest of the class are left dangling.

Stimulus-Boundedness and Thrusts. A *stimulus-bound* teacher cannot resist reacting to any stimulus that pops into his or her field of attention, even if the entire class is left dangling and waiting to continue. For example, while explaining a workbook assignment, the teacher suddenly asks, "What's that piece of paper doing on the floor? Jimmy, pick it up please." Or during the explanation of an arithmetic problem, "Sonja, you're slouching. Now sit up straight."

The highly similar *thrust* consists of the teacher's suddenly interrupting the children's activities with a statement or question, showing no regard for the children's current engagement or their readiness to receive the message. The teacher's own intent or desire is the only consideration. For example, during quiet seatwork, "Where's Bonnie today? Does anyone know why Bonnie isn't in school?"

Overdwelling. As the label suggests, a teacher can disrupt smoothness and momentum by dwelling on an issue far beyond what is necessary for children to understand. Kounin suggested that *nagging* and *preaching* are appropriate descriptors:

Richard, please stop talking. Some of you are cooperating and some of you are not. Ingrid is cooperating and doing her work, and so is Fred. Kirsten has not been listening. Now you all know this is not a playground. This is a classroom and we are supposed to be learning. Good citizens don't bother other children who are trying to learn, do they? So let's all cooperate and be good citizens and not disturb our classmates. You know it's hard to learn when there is a lot of noise . . .

Kounin's research confirmed that the smoother the movement between and within activities, the greater the academic engagement and the lower the deviancy. Arlin (1979) further confirmed that during transitions students' off-task behaviors— talking, hitting, throwing things, making distracting gestures or silly faces—occurred at a rate *double* the regular classroom rate.

Two recommendations for improving smoothness during transitions are to

1. Plan and structure the transitions in advance; that is, clearly instruct students regarding what they are to do next. For example, children can be drilled early in the year to put books back on the shelf or go to the gym calmly. If students know what they are to do during a transition, they usually will do it peacefully.

2. Establish clear expectations regarding what is and is not acceptable behavior during the transitions.

Emmer (1987) and Arlin (1979) added the following suggestions for improving smoothness and momentum within a lesson:

- Limit interruptions and intrusions.
- Begin and end activities as a group.
- Be certain that students know what they are supposed to be doing.
- Think through each learning task in terms of the demands placed on students and the points at which problems may be encountered.
- Be ready to redirect student attention and behavior when interest flags or distractions occur.

- Don't make children wait. One teacher with a reputation for good management gave this advice: "Never let kids wait longer than 1 minute for anything. You can't bog down or you'll pay for it!"

It is important to keep in mind that smoothness and momentum are maintained by most of the effective teaching practices to be described in Chapter 5: careful planning and good organization, including adequate directions, examples, and needed materials; high clarity; brisk pacing; monitoring progress; and selection of tasks that elicit high success rates.

Group Alerting

Another of Kounin's management principles was *group alerting*. Consider the following two sets of instructions:

"Jennifer, how much is 11 plus 12?"

"How much is 11 plus 12 (teacher pauses and looks around the room). Jennifer?"

Although they are obviously similar instructions, the first singles out Jennifer to think about and solve the problem. The rest of the students need not be alert; they can relax and wait until their names are called. The second instruction, however, has a strong group-alerting effect—no one knows who will be called on and so everyone must keep on his or her toes and be ready to respond. The same situation would arise if, say, students in a reading circle were called on in order, so that everyone knew exactly when they would need to begin thinking. All students would remain more alert if readers were selected in a more random fashion.

Group alerting then, refers to "those behaviors of a teacher that keep nonreciters on their toes while another child is reciting or before the selection of a new reciter" (Kounin, 1970). For example, the teacher can keep children in suspense by pausing and looking around to get children's attention and then saying, "Let's see now, who can . . . ?" A teacher also can call on different reciters randomly—so that no one knows who will be next—and change reciters frequently. The teacher can intersperse individual responses with unison responses or ask for a show of hands by all who know the correct answer. In addition, a teacher can alert nonreciters that they might have to react to what the reciter is doing. For example, they might be asked to find mistakes made by the reciter or they might be asked about the reciter's content.

A teacher might also increase anticipation and interest by saying something like "Let's put our thinking caps on; this might fool you" or adding new, novel, or alluring material to a recitation.

Kounin also warned of what he called *anti-group-alerting cues*—"behaviors of a teacher during a child's recitation, or preceding the selection of a new reciter, that reduce the involvement of nonreciters." A teacher should not change the focus of his or her attention away from the group, becoming immersed only in the performance of an individual reciter and directing questions and attention only to that individual as though the group were not there. A teacher should not select a reciter before the question is even stated or have reciters perform in a preselected order, for example, from left to right or around a circle.

As Kounin concluded, teachers who use a large number of group-alerting cues will get higher work engagement and less deviancy.

SATIATION VERSUS VARIETY: PLANNING FOR INTEREST

It is not surprising to learn that repetition and lack of variety lead to satiation and boredom and therefore to inattention, off-task behavior, and deviancy. Some signs of satiation and boredom include frequent and increasingly longer pauses in seatwork; looking around the room and out the window; and any number of student escape activities such as fiddling with paper clips, sharpening pencils, disturbing neighbors, drawing in books, and writing notes. On the other hand, satiation will occur more slowly if students feel they are making good progress and if the challenge, variety, and interest value of the lesson are strong. A number of effective methods for programming variety and challenge into the teaching routine are described in the following sections.

Variety in Activity and Content

A change in learning activity or content may be very small or it may be large and refreshing. Switching from copying spelling words to copying sentences is obviously trivial. In contrast, a change from copying spelling words to watching a thought-provoking science demonstration in another part of the room involves a change in content, location, group configuration, student activity and responsibility, props and materials, intellectual function, teacher function, and the child's overt behavior.

In a study of 58 elementary classes in 22 school districts, Stodolsky, Ferguson, and Wimpelberg (1981) identified the following 17 types of classroom activities:

Seatwork	Diverse seatwork
Individualized seatwork	Recitation
Discussion	Lecture
Demonstration	Checking work
Tests	Group work
Film or other audiovisual aids	Contests
	Giving instructions
Student reports	Tutoring
Preparation	Other

Besides the variety in activities, of course, there also is variety in content. *Content* is what the child would say was going on: "We're doing arithmetic" (reading, geography, science, handwriting, art, music, show-and-tell, etc.). Yinger's (1977) list of 53 activities compiled over a 2-week observation period included variation in both activity and content, for example,

Book reports	"Bucket check" (desk cleanup)
Reading laboratories	
Mathematics games	Library reading groups
Creative writing	Silent reading
Spelling bees	Mathematics units
Art	*Weekly Readers*
Cooking	Science units
Music (music teacher)	Assemblies
Movies	Field trips
Mindbenders (thinking skills)	Physical education
	Treats

There is little reason for a too-long and too-dreary involvement (or noninvolvement) with a single activity and content.

Variety in Level of Thinking

Different learning tasks elicit different types and levels of intellectual functioning. In increasing order of interest and intellectual challenge, Kounin (1970) pointed out that

- Only attention and perseverance are required for such tasks such as listening or copying simple material.

- Little more is required for practicing or using a simple skill, such as simple oral reading, coloring, easy addition, or recognition or naming.

- Comprehension and understanding are required, for example, for answering questions (orally or in writing), or recalling recently learned material.

- Thought and decision making are needed for solving arithmetic story problems, categorizing, or solving puzzles.

- Students might be asked to analyze, synthesize, evaluate, or think creatively, requiring maximum intellectual effort and engagement.

Materials and Audiovisual Aids

It is also possible to categorize materials and audiovisual aids according to the degree of interest or arousal they stimulate. At the routine and repetitive end of the scale are pencils, paper, and everyday books. Slightly more interesting are aids that, although generally available, are not used regularly, such as maps, charts, academic games, or songbooks. Still more attention getting are unique educational aids such as phonographs, movie or slide projectors, videotape players, microcomputers, microscopes, and new learning centers. Satiation and boredom should decrease with a larger variety of more interesting educational aids.

Group Configuration, Activities, and Responsibilities

The teacher can work with an entire class or a subgroup or have students work individually. Such changes in configuration can provide refreshing variety. Some *large-group* activities include the following:

Lectures, explanations, demonstrations by the teacher.

Teacher-led discussions.

Question-and-answer recitations (drilling, quizzing), perhaps with unison responses.

Sending students to the blackboard.

Presentations by individuals, groups, or panels.

Presentations via movies, videotapes, slides, filmstrips, cassette or other audiotapes, records.

Team games, simulations, role playing.

Brainstorming sessions.

Field trips.

Some *small-group* activities include

Reading groups.

Working together at learning centers.

Conducting experiments.

Attending to videotapes, records, and so forth.

Projects for planning and constructing.

Some *individual* learning activities include

Seatwork—mathematics, reading, art, and so forth.

Individual library research projects.

Working at learning centers.

Exploring bulletin boards, maps, displays, and so forth.

Location

Finally, a change in location also can reduce satiation. Students can work at their desks, around a table, in a reading circle, at a display or learning center, around the teacher, or outside the classroom in the instructional materials center, music room, art room, or gymnasium. Field trips, too, present a refreshing and memorable change of pace.

Kounin (1970) noted that variety in activity, content, level of thinking, props, and group configuration is most important for children in the lower elementary grades. For upper-elementary and older children, feelings of progress become increasingly important in preventing satiation and boredom. Overall, however, as Kounin put it, programming "to reduce satiation by learning-related variety is a significant dimension of classroom management."

PHYSICAL ARRANGEMENTS

Some room arrangements are more conducive than others to manageability. The principles are few, but solid. Basically, seating should be arranged to maximize student attention, minimize distraction and disruption, and enable the teacher to monitor the class visually at all times. The teacher should face the class, whether seated at the desk or standing. Students should face the teacher at times when attention is expected. Students' chairs should not face windows (Emmer, 1987). Small groups should be located so they do not distract the rest of the class. If several groups are working, they should be spread out to reduce disruptions and distractions. When working with a small group, the teacher should face the remainder of the class.

Traffic patterns also should be analyzed. Are main entrance and exit routes wide enough and free of obstacles? Can students get to the bookshelves, wastebasket, supply areas, teacher's desk, or pencil sharpener without distracting others, tripping over the guinea pig, or stepping on someone's artwork or lunch? Such free paths are especially important for handicapped students in the classroom. Emmer (1987) made the following recommendations:

1. Student seating should be arranged to permit easy monitoring by the teacher and to avoid distractions to the students.

2. Clear lines of sight should be maintained from every student's seat to the instructional areas.

3. Frequently used areas should be easily accessible.

4. Traffic lanes should be kept free of obstructions.

5. Equipment and materials should be arranged so that they are readily accessible to the students or the teacher.

One line of research has suggested that increased spatial density (crowdedness) produces distractibility, inattention, off-task behavior, dissatisfaction, aggression, and a reduction in positive social interaction (Shapiro, 1975; Silverstein, 1979). Other research has confirmed, as we suspected all along, that front-and-center seating improves attitudes, participation, and achievement (Weinstein, 1979).

BEGINNING THE YEAR: CLIMATE, RULES, AND GROOVING STUDENTS

Sometimes experienced teachers will advise the newcomer to get tough immediately and ease up later: "Don't smile until Christmas." Such an approach is fine for teachers who wish to become the enemy, establishing in the first hour perhaps a year-long relationship of alienation, mistrust, and hostility. A better idea, according to Good and Brophy (1977), is the early establishment of likeability, credibility, respectability, trustworthiness, and being a generally attractive and worthwhile person. Good student–teacher relationships and positive interactions promote good student attitudes (Brophy, 1982; Purkey & Novak, 1984). However, it is important to remember that the main goal is to teach, not to be a buddy.

Climate

Good and Brophy (1977) recommended that teachers establish a friendly yet businesslike and academic climate by communicating to students that they enjoy teaching, both the instruction and the personal interaction; they look forward to getting to know each student individually; they are willing to help not only with subject matter, but in any way they can; they expect to teach the subject matter successfully and to help each student go as far as he or she can. Teachers are teachers, not disciplinarians. Certain student behaviors will be expected; others will be forbidden.

According to Charles (1983), the psychosocial environment is much more important to achievement, self-concept, and school attitudes than is the physical environment. The teacher therefore must try to create and maintain a psychosocial environment that is pleasant, warm, and supportive. Such an environment includes clear achievement and behavior expectations, good planning and structure, and maintenance of control. The teacher also can plan activities to help students become better acquainted and work together cooperatively.

A number of recent studies have focused on the importance of beginning-of-the-year activities, especially clarifying expectations for student behavior and establishing norms and a climate consistent with those expectations (e.g., Anderson, Evertson, & Emmer, 1980, 1982; Emmer, Evertson, & Anderson, 1980; Evertson, Emmer, Clements, Sanford, & Worsham, 1984; Emmer, Evertson, Sanford, Clements, & Worsham, 1984). Emmer (1987) concluded that "if the teacher is uncertain about what behaviors are or are not acceptable in different types of activities, student behavior that is counterproductive and difficult to change may become established."

Teachers can establish norms by praising appropriate behavior and providing corrective feedback for incorrect behavior. More direct methods include presenting formal rules and procedures that regulate classroom behavior and work requirements. Generally, students must believe that their teachers intend to remain in control of the classroom, and that they mean what they say.

Rules

Setting rules, explaining the reasons behind the rules, and correcting the situation when rules are violated contribute much to the academic and orderly climate necessary for learning. Rules should be simple and clear, and they must be enforced equitably for all students. The children should understand that the rules will help them and the teacher work together as a team. If the rules are violated, teamwork is disrupted and time is wasted. Specific rules will depend on the grade level and general level of rebelliousness in a class. Obviously, rules for first-graders will differ from rules for junior high or high school students, and rules for college-bound middle-class students will be different from rules for students in high-crime neighborhoods.

One effective tactic is to involve students themselves in the rule making. They will be more likely to feel that the rules are fair, and they will have an intrinsic commitment to abide by their own rules (Emmer, Evertson, Sanford, Clements, & Worsham, 1984).

As a general principle, rules should be broad, flexible, and few in number (Good & Brophy, 1977). Some general rules might be as follows:

- Disruptive behaviors will not be tolerated.

- We will be courteous at all times.

- Listen carefully when others speak.

- There is to be no talking during seatwork.

- We will change from one learning activity to another as quickly and quietly as possible.

Of course, classrooms are complex, with a large variety of activities and grouping patterns. Consequently, the formulation of expectations—as well as the concrete rules and procedures that embody those expectations—also is complex. Emmer (1987) recommended that teachers formulate expectations and plan rules and procedures related to activities and work requirements in several areas. In the category of teaching and learning activities, rules are needed for

- Whole-class presentations.

- Teacher-led small groups, including expectations for students not in the group.

- Independent small-group or project work.

- Individual seatwork.

In the area of procedures, rules are needed for

- Obtaining assistance when the teacher is occupied with a small group or an individual.

- Entering and leaving the room, including returning from a resource, art, or music room.

- Making transitions between activities.

- Room and equipment use.

- Grading procedures and related recordkeeping.

According to Emmer (1987), rules also are needed to guide the following areas related to work completion and accountability:

- Make-up work and other procedures related to student absences.

- Completing assignments.

- Assisting students who encounter difficulty with their assignments.

- Dealing with students who fail to complete their work.

- Providing feedback to students about their progress.

Emmer pointed out that at the secondary level students have learned more so-called going-to-school skills, and so there are fewer procedural concerns. At the elementary level, however, teachers especially need to clarify their expectations and establish norms related to all of the types of activities and procedures listed here.

Grooving Students

Smith and Geoffrey (1968) coined the phrase *grooving the students* to refer to an effective beginning-of-the-year management strategy. Basically, the teacher asks students individually or as a group to perform relatively innocuous tasks and errands in order to establish the idea that teachers give orders and students follow them. Berliner (1986a) said that "our expert teachers had almost all learned to groove the students, though none of them had a label for that kind of knowledge."

HANDLING MISBEHAVIOR

Ideally—with emphasis on the *ideal*—an effective, successful teacher would create a good academic atmosphere and good school attitudes, maintain high academic engagement, and successfully manage the classroom to prevent inattentive, off-task, and disruptive behavior. Realistically, however, misbehavior will occur and the teacher must plan in advance for handling it.

As a core principle, Emmer (1987) stressed that "the key to good discipline is preventing inappropriate behavior in the first place, and when it occurs dealing with it promptly and relatively unobtrusively before it escalates or intensifies."

Punishment

Punishment is the creation of negative consequences. Classroom forms of punishment include withholding privileges or other rewards, using a penalty system, disapproving or criticizing, requiring restitution, assigning additional work, isolating the student in a stimulation-free area (time out), or detaining the student in an in-school suspension room (see Inset 4-1).

The effects of punishment have intrigued psychologists for decades. Consider some of the complexities of punishment:

1. Punishment can be physically or psychologically painful.

2. Punishment such as shouting at a student usually does not eliminate the behavior; it just slows (suppresses) it temporarily.

3. Punishment by itself does not necessarily show the student what the appropriate behavior should be.

4. The teacher's verbal (or physical) aggression serves as a poor model for impressionable youngsters. The teacher who screams, "Sit down and shut up! I'll teach you to yell in the halls!" certainly will.

5. Punishment frequently produces undesirable side effects such as fear, anxiety, resentment, mistrust, hostility, or aggressiveness and a thorough dislike for the teacher and school in general. The negative attitudes may lead to further troublesome avoidance and escape behaviors such as lying, cheating on tests, playing hooky, or dropping out of school entirely. Punishment can provide a good excuse for students *not* to change their deviant ways (Emmer, 1987). As Kounin (1970) noted, when students like the teacher, they also like the class; and when they like the teacher and the class, they are more highly motivated to achieve.

6. The effects of punishment are unpredictable, depending on student personality. Some students, especially those who are more confident and secure, may accept firm corrections and constructive criticism well. However, anxious and insecure students respond better to positive reinforcers. For some students, punishment is *rewarding*—glares and reprimands produce just the reinforcing attention they were looking for. If time-out areas or in-school suspension rooms are not used, getting sent to the principal's office permits the offender to see exciting injuries and school visitors and watch secretaries run the copying machine and operate the intercom. The culprit might even get to run errands.

INSET 4–1

Time Out and Suspension Rooms

The time-out strategy is one that is acceptable to most parents and principals and usually is effective in calming down a rowdy or misbehaving elementary school child. Currently, it is used primarily—although not entirely—with special education students. Basically, the student is sent to a stimulation-free area or time-out room for 2, 5, or perhaps 10 or 15 minutes. The time-out area must be free of high-interest stimulation—no windows; no secretaries to watch; no lunch bags to plunder; no equipment to fiddle with; and no attractive magazines, posters, or calendars. The student is to calm down and think about his or her behavior, not earn a refreshing change of scenery.

Many junior and senior high schools have created in-school monitored suspension rooms that are used for short periods during the day, as well as for all-day detentions. The suspension rooms operate in basically the same way as time-out areas, except that teachers or supervisors monitor the room on a rotating basis. The suspended students are expected to continue working as if they were attending their normal classes.

As for physical punishment, some states legally prohibit it while others allow it. Before striking a student, however, the teacher should consider not only the six points just listed but also the reactions of parents, school board members, the principal, other students, other teachers, and perhaps his or her own conscience. A calm, professionally prepared teacher should have other alternatives, including other punishment alternatives, prepared in advance. A regretful slap or shaking need never be considered.

It is true that punishment sometimes is needed, usually because a serious infraction occurs regardless of a teacher's best efforts. Some examples might be physical aggression, intimidation, verbal abuse, damage to property, or disruptive behavior that continues despite attempts to stop or redirect it.

Emmer (1987) itemized the following five general principles relating to using punishment in the classroom:

1. Whenever possible, the punishment should be logically related to the misbehavior. For example, if property is destroyed, restitution in the form of repair or replacement is logical. If a mess is made, it should be cleaned up. Excessive chatter may result in the loss of talking privileges.

2. Moderate punishment might be as effective as severe punishment. For example, 5 or 10 minutes of time out might be as effective with elementary students as a half hour; missing one 10-minute recess may be as effective as a half-hour detention after school.

3. Punishment procedures should focus on helping a student understand the problem and eliciting a commitment to better behavior. According to Emmer, students should be confronted with the unacceptable behavior and permitted to made a commitment to improvement. One good strategy is for the student to acknowledge the poor behavior in writing, including a written agreement to change, and have the document signed by a parent or guardian.

4. Punishment should not be overused with regard to either duration or frequency. Some easy-to-use punishment systems include the use of fines, extra busywork such as writing sentences or copying a passage, withholding privileges, time out, or a demerit system whereby the teacher records misbehavior with checks (demerits). With this system, when a certain number of checks has accumulated, a penalty such as detention is assessed. The system has the advantage of providing plenty of warning before a punishment actually is imposed.

The danger with these punishment systems is that because of their simplicity, teachers can easily overuse them, instead of relying on more positive approaches such as redirecting. Indeed, some secondary teachers use punishment systems (e.g., assessing a fine or assigning detention for tardiness) as an ongoing classroom policy, finding punishment easier and quicker than trying to deter behavior with more positive approaches. However, overusing punishment causes the classroom climate to degenerate as the teacher focuses more and more on catching students misbehaving. Students become resentful, and lessons are interrupted each time a student is nabbed.

5. Consistency is essential. A teacher cannot assign penalties for excessive talking one day, then ignore it the next. Unexplained inconsistency in enforcing rules will cause some students to raise their levels of misbehavior.

In all cases of punishment, the teacher should make it clear that it is the poor behavior that is the focus of attention, not the student as a person. The behavior must change; the person is fine. Teachers must especially avoid publicly humiliating students, which damages both student attitudes and classroom climate.

The teacher's credibility for fairness also is critical—both in treating everyone the same and in fitting the punishment to the infraction.

Ignoring, Vicarious Learning, and Humor

For many minor rule infractions such as not paying attention or speaking out without raising hands, one time-tested strategy is to *ignore* the offense and reward correct behavior. The behavior-modification-based approach should teach Bobby Blurtwell that speaking out or interrupting others will get him nothing, while the correct behavior of raising his hand produces good results. As a caution, the ignoring strategy at first might cause a student to increase the disruptiveness, just as a customer might raise his or her voice when ignored by a store clerk.

Another positive strategy is *vicarious learning,* or modeling. The teacher can shape behavior by rewarding other students for behaving properly ("I like the way Freddy raises his hand before speaking. That's how we do things in school.").

A *humorous* response to a rule infraction also might control the behavior, and without resentment or other ill feelings. "You have a lovely voice Bobby, but I'd rather not hear it until I call on you. Is that a deal?" Such a response conveys the message, and everyone stays pleasant and unperturbed.

Problem–Centered Negotiations and Investigations

Many students who will not respond to either positive appeals or punishment will agree to change their ways in a face-to-face negotiated settlement. The teacher arranges for a private discussion, probably after school. The teacher can ask the student for his or her explanation of the misbehavior. The teacher then provides feedback in terms of personal reactions ("I get very upset because you won't let me teach my class") and the effects on the rest of the class ("You disturb everyone and keep them from reading and doing their lessons"). The problem-centered discussion should be honest and open and have a no-lose character; that is, the agreement should be satisfactory to both parties with no loss of face and no obvious winner or loser. The teacher, of course, is the clear winner if the negotiated truce works.

Occasionally, problems will arise among students that require investigation (e.g., accusations of theft). It is important for the teacher to establish a reputation for fairness. The discussion should be private, including only those involved, and it should have a problem-solving focus: What is the problem and how shall we resolve it?

Each student must be given an uninterrupted opportunity to present his or her side of the story. The teacher also should try to help each understand the motives and perceptions of the other person. Often, students discover that what they perceived as an infringement on their rights actually was a misunderstanding. If someone is guilty of a crime (theft, obscenities, shoving, etc.), that person should leave the meeting understanding that the punishment or reprimand is due to his or her own behavior, not the teacher's hostility or personal dislike. Hopefully, the student should be ashamed, embarrassed, and unlikely to repeat the offense.

A significant side effect of problem-centered negotiations and investigations is that all students in the class learn that if they misbehave they will have to account to the teacher personally and face-to-face.

In cases where serious misbehavior recurs, a long-term solution is likely to include consultation with parents and planning with other school personnel such as the principal or assistant principal, the special education teacher, a counselor, and/or the school psychologist.

MANAGEMENT AND DISCIPLINE IN DISADVANTAGED NEIGHBORHOODS

A teacher's authority will be tested in virtually any classroom. With disadvantaged children, the tests will come quickly: How much talking will the teacher tolerate? Can I get away with bursting in 5 minutes late? Can I wear sunglasses in class? Can I take a nap? Can

I get away with stomping and chattering to the pencil sharpener? Disruptive students are hoping the teacher will fail in his or her attempts to cope with them. However, they also will lose respect for the too-tolerant teacher and probably will feel more insecure in the classroom. Moreover, students who are watching usually hope the teacher will handle the rascal properly. If not, they too will lose respect for the teacher and eventually may turn against him or her. The teacher obviously cannot afford to fail.

New York City psychologist Allan Ornstein (1969) itemized nearly two dozen experience-based guidelines for controlling classroom rowdiness and improving learning. While Ornstein specifically worked with difficult-to-control, difficult-to-teach students, his list contains good ideas for classroom management of other students as well. According to Ornstein, "Some of the rules . . . seem almost too basic for explanation. Yet my experience is that they are far from rudimentary." We have classified them as *daily routines, teacher–student interactions,* and *discipline.*

Daily Routines

1. The first rule is to have rules.

2. Train students to enter the room in an orderly fashion. They are there to learn.

3. Require 100% attention before starting. Do not wait for an offender to pay attention when he or she feels like it.

4. Do not permit students to abuse hall passes with frequent so-called emergencies.

5. The teacher may wish to prohibit students from wandering or coming to the teacher's desk. If students remain in their seats, discipline problems will be reduced.

6. Be certain to dismiss the class. Students should work to the end of the class; they should not start packing up before being instructed to do so. However, students are in no mood to work after the bell.

7. Be consistent with class routine. Many students do not cope well with changes.

Teacher–Student Interactions

8. Get to know students early in the term. Do not let them believe they are shielded by anonymity. The teacher also should know the difficulties and limitations of each student.

9. Speak softly, do not shout, and try not to get excited.

10. Be clear with instructions and give one instruction at a time. Make sure each instruction is understood and executed before issuing another one.

11. Keep students engaged in meaningful activity. Use interest to maintain order. A bored class is potential trouble.

12. Aim for full class participation. Teach students to show respect for one another by listening to one another.

13. Be aware of undercurrents of behavior. While teaching, try to watch what everyone is doing. Try not to turn your back on the class.

14. Hold students accountable. Students must realize they cannot get away with poor preparation, neglecting homework, or habitual tardiness.

15. Keep a clean and attractive room. Gaping closet doors and diarrayed papers and chairs set a tone of disorder. Change pictures and bulletin boards. All of this shows you care.

16. Be friendly but maintain a proper psychological distance. It is fine to make a joke and to be an entertainer. However, students may perceive a too-friendly teacher as "soft" and take advantage of him or her. They prefer to keep the teacher on a different level.

Discipline
17. Be consistent with discipline. Do not be lenient one day, strict the next. Do not punish one student and not another. All threatened punishment must be carried out.

18. Do not make impossible threats ("Stop that or I'll have you expelled in 10 minutes!"). The teacher loses credibility with such warnings.

19. Be flexible. Some children need guidance, not strict discipline. Others need both. Some excitable students must be handled after class; others can be dealt with on the spot.

20. Do not punish the whole class for the offenses of an individual. It causes resentment and shows you cannot cope. Try to invoke peer disapproval by explaining that "Some person is disrupting the class."

21. Never make an offense personal. Try to make the disruptions appear aimed at the class ("Peter, you're ruining it for the class").

22. Avoid public arguments; they make a hero of the debater.

Readers should recognize many of these principles, which have appeared earlier in this chapter. Ornstein has emphasized, modified, and extended them to apply to students who might be more difficult to manage.

SUMMARY

Good classroom management aims at increasing engagement and reducing disruptions. It is essential for good achievement, behavior, and attitudes. Classroom management, or good discipline, is largely preventative.

Causes of disruptiveness include such factors as poverty, low ability, emotional problems, and peer influence, among others.

Principles of good management have been placed in categories of *rules and expectations* (establish positive expectations, clear rules, withitness, accountability); *classroom organization* (arrange for continual surveillance, efficient transitions between activities, and high interest; and remove stimuli that set off talking and clowning); *classroom activities* (start class quickly and purposefully, keep students engaged, let students know what to do when finished); and *responses to misbehavior* (ignore minor deviancy; use humor or threats first; if needed, administer punishment quickly, fairly, and in a way that is focused on the behavior).

Kounin's (1970) *withitness* is letting students know that the teacher knows what is going on. The target and timing of reprimands must be appropriate. According to Emmer (1987), withitness involves close monitoring and prompt handling of inappropriate behavior.

Overlapping is handling two classroom matters at once, for instance, attending to deviancy without disrupting a learning activity. Another strategy for handling misbehavior is to redirect students from inappropriate to appropriate behaviors. Momentum, keeping the class moving, and smoothness, the absence of teacher behaviors that produce "jerky" movement, are also important to good classroom management. Smoothness and momentum can be disrupted by flip-flops, fragmentation, dangles, stimulus-boundedness and thrusts, and overdwelling. Smoothness can be increased by planning transitions, establishing clear expectations, not making children wait, and using effective teaching practices.

Group alerting is another technique teachers can use to help keep all students attentive. To reduce boredom, teachers should plan variety in activity and content, level of thinking, materials and audiovisual aids, group configuration, and location. Physical arrangements should maximize student attention, minimize distraction, permit visual monitoring, and allow traffic movement.

At the beginning of the year, it is better for teachers to establish likeability and respectability than to get tough. Early establishment of expectations for high achievement and good behavior are important for a good psychosocial environment.

Setting rules that are simple, clear, broad, and flexible will increase orderliness; students can help make the rules. Each learning activity will require its own rules and procedures.

Grooving students means establishing the idea that teachers give orders and students follow them, in accordance with the core notion that misbehavior is best prevented in the first place. When misbehavior does occur, it should be dealt with promptly, unobtrusively, and fairly.

Punishment may be physical or psychological, just suppresses the behavior, may not teach appropriate substitute behavior, presents a bad model, affects different students differently, and can produce many negative side-effects. Two forms of punishment, time out and suspension rooms, seem to be effective and acceptable discipline methods.

Punishment should be related to the misbehavior. It should be moderate, not severe or overused. It should help the student commit to improved behavior, be administered in a consistent way, and focus on the behavior rather than the person.

Ignoring, vicarious learning, and humor are alternatives to punishment. Problem-centered negotiations and investigations are also effective in controlling misbehavior.

Ornstein itemized 22 guidelines for classroom management in disadvantaged neighborhoods, which we placed in the categories of *daily routines* (e.g., have rules, be consistent with class routines), *teacher–student interactions* (e.g., get to know students, be clear with instructions, engage students in meaningful activity), and *discipline* (e.g., be flexible, be consistent, do not make impossible threats).

Chapter Five

Effective Teachers

This literature is theoretically, methodologically, and practically rich. It promises a conceptualization of conditions in schools that plausibly support learning to teach and the steady improvement of teaching over time.
—Judith W. Little, "Teachers as Colleagues"

The 1980s [is] an extraordinary time in the history of research on teaching.
—Herbert J. Walberg, "Syntheses of Research on Teaching"

We have looked at characteristics of effective principals and effective schools, which, taken together, point up the importance of an academic atmosphere, high expectations, a safe and orderly environment, supervising and training teachers, high engagement rates, emphasis on basics, monitoring student progress, good classroom management practices, and many other specifics. Virtually all of these factors improve student achievement, behavior, and attitudes through what teachers do in their classrooms. The bottom line in effective schooling is effective teaching.

Before turning to teacher characteristics and teaching patterns that contribute to student achievement, we should comment briefly on one issue that weighs heavily on the value of this chapter. Some critics of research on effective teaching have pointed out that statistical correlations between most individual teaching variables and measures of achievement are quite low (e.g., Dunkin & Biddle, 1984); that is, they are said not to be very important. There are two replies. First, as Gage (1978, 1985) carefully explained and as we mentioned in Chapter 3, even weak relationships can make important differences. Using a medical example of men who had suffered one heart attack, Gage explained how a drug called propranolol led to a 93.0% survival rate after 30 months, compared with a 90.5% survival rate for those given a placebo. This tiny 2.5% advantage has led to the saving of about 21,000 lives per year in the United States alone. As Gage pointed out, "Correlations . . . do not need to be large in order to be important . . . we are influencing dropout rates, literacy, placement in special classes, love of learning, self-esteem, and the holistic ability to integrate many facts and concepts in a complex way."

Second, it also is true that the effects of variables known to improve achievement are *additive*. Many small improvements can add up to a worthwhile total change in student achievement with accompanying improvements in attitudes and behavior. An individual teacher concerned with professional improvement or a serious school-wide improvement program will work toward not just one or two changes, but many. For example, a knowledgeable improvement program might seek to adopt all five of the basic characteristics of effective schools described by Weber and by Edmonds: strong instructional leadership, a school-wide academic focus and climate, expectations that all students are able to learn and will do so, an instructional emphasis on basic skills, and close monitoring of progress. In addition, many other confirmed correlates of effectiveness can be adopted, for example, those related to effective principals (Chapter 2), good management practices (Chapter 4), and effective teachers (this chapter). The South Carolina Education Improvement Act, for example, includes dozens of these and other changes, and achievement has shown "steady improvement since 1983" (T. Peterson, 1988).

A school-wide effort by administrators and by energetic, dedicated teachers to improve school effectiveness is almost certain to make a difference in student achievement.

In this chapter we first review variables and teaching behaviors that promote achievement primarily because they increase academic engagement. Next, we summarize variables related to another pivotal concept in teaching effectiveness: organizing and structuring the learning experiences to increase clarity and efficiency and reduce ambiguity. Finally, we itemize briefly other variables that are pertinent to effective teaching.

In addition, as integrative reviews that are partially redundant with ideas presented both in earlier chapters and in this one, principles of effective teaching assembled by effective schooling leaders Anderson, Evertson, and Brophy, Rosenshine, and the Beginning Teacher Evaluation Study are summarized along with suggestions by Madeline Hunter for improving teaching.

ACADEMIC ENGAGEMENT

Science has confirmed beyond any reasonable doubt that academic engagement—time on task—is indeed the single most crucial factor contributing to student achievement. Many of the variables noted in earlier chapters improve achievement by directly or indirectly increasing students' academic engagement. For example, the vision of the principal and the academic climate of the school orient teachers toward spending more time teaching content and students toward spending more time studying and learning.

The importance and centrality attributed to academic engagement in the effective-teaching literature led to Erickson's (1986) exaggerated charge that "over the 1970s and into the 1980s, the job of the teacher was seen [only] as keeping learners on task."

Academic learning time (ALT) is a more sophisticated interpretation of the interrelated ideas of allocated time (time allowed) and academic engaged time (time on task). ALT is more highly related to measures of student achievement than is engaged time. ALT is defined as "time engaged with materials or activities related to the outcome measure being used (often an achievement test), during which a student experiences a high success rate" (Berliner, 1984).

Figure 5-1, prepared by Berliner, illustrates how the total amount of *allocated time* (AT) may be reduced to *engaged time* (ET), which is the amount of allocated time that students actually spend on task. Furthermore, only part of the engaged time is spent working on material directly related to the test content *(time related to outcome,* or TRO). Allocated time, engaged time, or time related to outcome measures can yield low, medium, or high success rates for students. As shown in (e) in Figure 5-1, only the portion of the allocated time that is time engaged in activities related to the outcome measures and that provides students with a high success rate is classed as *academic learning time* (ALT).

FIGURE 5–1

Academic Learning Time

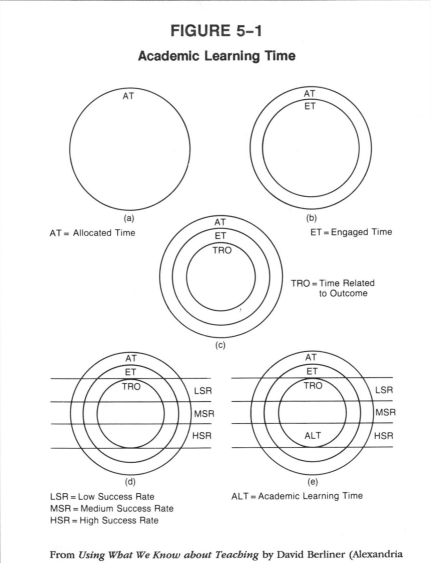

From *Using What We Know about Teaching* by David Berliner (Alexandria VA: ASCD, 1984, p. 61). Copyright © 1984 Association for Supervision and Curriculum Development. Reprinted by permission of the publisher and David Berliner.

As Berliner has pointed out, ALT has very practical implications for improving teaching. For example, consider imaginary student Jimmy, who in October is at the 50th percentile in reading. If Jimmy were to experience an average amount of ALT (23 minutes per day, Berliner estimates), his reading proficiency would remain at about the 50th percentile by December. However, if Jimmy experienced only about 4 minutes per day of ALT, his standing in December would drop to about the 39th percentile. Conversely, if ALT were increased to about 52 minutes per day, Jimmy's reading would be predicted to climb to about the 66th percentile by December.

The concept of ALT can improve teachers' understanding of when time on task will and will not lead to measured improvements in achievement; that is, the students must be engaged at a high success rate with activities related to the outcome measure (test).

ALLOCATED TIME, OPPORTUNITY TO LEARN, AND AMOUNT OF CONTENT COVERED

Allocated time, opportunity to learn, and the amount of content covered are closely related to each other, to academic engagement, and to achievement in basic skills (Berliner, 1984, 1985, 1986a; Brophy & Good, 1985; Cohen, 1987; Rosenshine, 1979; U.S. Department of Education, 1986, 1987; Walberg, 1985). Note that time allocations, opportunities for learning, and content coverage all could be increased by lengthening the school day or the school year. Some foreign countries have longer school days and years (Walberg, 1984). However, research on effective schooling strongly suggests that many teachers simply need to make better use of the time they have.

Elementary school teachers have strong control over their time allocations and use, and there are large differences among teachers in the amounts of time they allocate to different subjects and topics. For example, the Beginning Teacher Evaluation Study (Denham & Lieberman, 1980; Fisher et al., 1978) discovered that among just five second-grade teachers the time allocated for reading and language arts ranged from 47 to 118 minutes per day—a maximum difference of 71 minutes per day. Similarly, a group of fifth-grade teachers allocated from 68 to 137 minutes per day for reading and language arts, a maximum difference of 69 minutes per day. With mathematics instruction, one second-grade teacher allocated just 16 minutes per day while another allocated 51 minutes. Such dramatic differences in time allocations should be interpreted not as unique cases but as representative examples.

The total-year differences among these classes with regard to students' opportunity to learn is nothing short of staggering. Subtracting holidays, field trips, outings, and end-of-the-year days from the 180-day school year leaves about 120 school days that are available for instruction in earnest. Multiplying 16 minutes of mathematics times 120 days produces a total allocation of just 1,920 minutes (32 hours), compared with 5,640 minutes (94 hours) of mathematics for students who receive 51 minutes of instruction in it daily. As Berliner (1984) observed, "Such marked variability in time . . . leads, inevitably, to differences in achievement."

Much research supports the intuitively sound principle that achievement is related to opportunities for learning. Jane Stallings and her colleagues (Stallings, 1986; Stallings & Kaskowitz, 1974; Stallings, Cory, Fairweather, & Needels, 1977, 1978) confirmed that, indeed, when more time is spent on mathematics and reading instruction, scores in those subjects are higher. Conversely, they found that basic skills achievement scores were negatively related to the amount of classroom time spent on stories, music, dance, arts and crafts, group sharing, socializing, and games (including academic games). *No nonacademic activity produced positive correlations with achievement.* Furthermore, teaching patterns in which teachers worked mostly with one or two individuals, rather than teaching formal lessons to the entire class, also depressed average class achievement.

In Stallings's research, at both elementary and secondary levels, the key factor most strongly correlated with achievement was simply *quantity* of instruction. The greater the amount of content covered, the higher were achievement scores. So central are content coverage, time allocations, and opportunities for learning that Stallings (1986) labeled her teacher training project the Effective Use of Time Program. The program dealt entirely with coaching teachers to make better use of available time.

A major conclusion of Stallings and Kaskowitz (1974) was that students will make greater achievement gains if they spend most of their time either being directly instructed by the teacher or working independently under close teacher supervision. They recommended spending more time with groups, especially the entire class; spending less time either uninvolved or involved with individuals; giving more instruction; asking more questions; and providing more feedback. As a format for these changes, they recommended the traditional recitation pattern of *teacher questions* (direct, factual questions rather than more open, higher level questions) followed by *student responses* and *teacher feedback*.

In addition to time spent on the nonacademic activities mentioned earlier, Stallings (1986) noted other factors that are *negatively* related to achievement—factors that bear directly on this topic of opportunity to learn. Achievement is lower when the teacher does not interact with students; the teacher spends time getting organized rather than teaching; students are offered choices of activities; time is lost to outside interruptions; students spend time socializing or otherwise not cooperating; or students work independently on silent reading or written assignments for long periods of time. Stallings (1986) noted that "past studies indicate that low-achieving students are off-task most during lengthy seatwork assignments."

In Stallings's Effective Use of Time Program, teachers were coached in increasing student interest and attention—academic engagement. For example, the teachers were taught to vary activities, perhaps by arranging class time to include some teacher explanation, some reading, some writing, and some discussion. They were encouraged to increase students' involvement, for example, by having them make notes on each others' speeches. The teachers also learned to watch for and reduce disruptions and intrusions from the outside.

As for allocating class time, based on time-use patterns of highly effective teachers, Stallings recommended that about 15% of class time be used for organizing (making assignments, classroom management, or the teacher organizing alone), 50% be used for interactive instruction (instruction/explanation, discussion/review of assignments, reading aloud, practice/drill, or taking tests), and 35% be used in monitoring silent reading or written work. No time should be spent in social interaction with students, students being uninvolved, or students being disciplined.

Viewing classroom time in terms of interaction percentages, Stallings recommended that what she called "academic statements" should comprise about 80% of all interactions, "organizing or management statements" about 15%, "behavior statements" 3%, and "social statements" 2%. There should be no interactions described by Stallings as "student shout-outs," "student refusals to answer," "teacher involved with visitor," or "negative interactions."

When we think about opportunities for learning and content coverage, we also should think about the selection of specific curriculum content. Such content is only partly determined by school district policies and guidelines. Teachers make the final content decisions, and there are dramatic differences among teachers' choices. In one extreme case, an elementary teacher taught absolutely nothing about fractions over a 90-day observation period. When asked for an explanation, she replied very simply, "I don't like fractions" (Berliner, 1984). The impact on her students' mastery of fractions need not be explained.

One study showed, perhaps not surprisingly, that teachers' decisions about content are influenced by (a) the perceived *effort* required to teach a subject matter area, (b) the perceived *difficulty for students,* and (c) the teachers' *personal feelings of enjoyment* while teaching that subject matter area (Schwille et al., 1983). An elementary teacher who enjoyed teaching science taught 28 times more science than a teacher who conceded that she did not enjoy the subject. A first-grade teacher who felt that reading was the preeminent content area to be taught spent almost all available class time on reading. Her students' feelings of personal competence became tied to their accomplishments as readers. Content decisions clearly have powerful impacts on opportunity to learn and, therefore, on achievement.

There are many other factors noted in the literature on effective schooling that aid learning by increasing time allocations, opportunity to learn, and content coverage. For example, principals and teachers should make the need for learning time part of school climate and culture. Time-use allocations among subjects taught should be established and followed. Everyone—administration, staff, and students—should understand these time-use priorities. Administrators should organize the school calendar to provide maximum learning time. School events should be scheduled to avoid disruption of learning time. New instructional programs and school procedures should be evaluated according to their potential impact on learning time. Student pullouts from regular classes (e.g., early dismissal for the tennis team) should be minimized or eliminated through monitoring and, if necessary, corrective action. Unassigned time and time spent on noninstructional activities should be minimized. Extra learning time should be provided for students who need or want it; the extra help should be available outside of regular school hours if necessary.

ACTIVE TEACHING
AND MAINTAINING A BRISK PACE

Maintaining a brisk pace is a recurrent characteristic of effective teachers (Anderson, Evertson, & Brophy, 1982; Brophy, 1979). Keeping instruction moving at a good pace sustains interest, increases engagement, and permits teachers to cover plenty of content. Barr (1980), for example, discovered that a full 80% of the differences among children in basal reading achievement was due to the pace of instruction. Another study found that teachers of higher achieving children did indeed move more briskly through the curriculum, covering 1.13 pages of fourth-grade mathematics per day compared with .71 pages per day for teachers of lower achieving children (Good, Grouws, & Beckerman, 1978).

Student ability level also is involved. Not surprisingly, with faster learning students (or easier material), the pacing may be brisker, larger steps may be used, less review is needed, and more time can be spent on new material. Slower students require a slower pace, smaller steps, more review, more explanation of new material, more guided practice, and more independent practice (Rosenshine, 1986). Teachers do indeed pace low- and high-ability groups dramatically differently—with the high groups paced as much as 15 times faster than the low groups (Shavelson, 1983). Content coverage therefore can be as much as 15 times greater for the high groups. The problem with adjusting the learning pace to accommodate ability differences is that slower learning students will cover less content, unless additional time is found.

In a study of junior high school English and mathematics teachers of lower ability students, Evertson and colleagues (1980) concluded that maintaining a brisk pace in these grades is even more important to high achievement than it is in the elementary grades. Berliner (1984) concluded that "the more a teacher covers, the more students learn . . . [and] . . . evidence for the power of the pacing variable keeps mounting."

Some factors that contribute to active teaching and maintaining a brisk pace include starting class quickly and purposefully and ending lessons or class promptly. The teacher can use clear start and stop cues to help pace lessons according to specific time targets. Reviews, activities, assignment materials, and supplies should be ready when students arrive. Administrative matters (roll taking, announcements, etc.) should be handled with quick, efficient routines that minimize class disruption. New objectives can be introduced quickly. Transitions between activities should be smooth and rapid. Students also can be encouraged to work at a reasonably brisk pace.

One problem worth considering in regard to maintaining a brisk pace (and covering extensive content) is its possible cost in the development of thinking skills. Creativity, critical thinking, and Bloom's (1974) higher taxonomic level skills require extensive processing time, for example, when a teacher poses questions requiring analysis, synthesis, or evaluation. Independent projects such as a classroom newspaper, play writing and production, or a science research project may not cover content at a brisk pace, but there will be gains in skills such as creative problem solving, inquiry, critical thinking, evaluation, and independent learning (Davis & Rimm, 1989).

CLASS SIZE

Another finding, logically related to those already covered, is that achievement is slightly negatively related to class size. Fewer students in a class means higher achievement (Smith & Glass, 1980; Stallings et al., 1977; Walberg, 1985). Crawford (1983) explained that with smaller student—teacher ratios, teachers can move through curricula faster, provide more individualized tutorial instruction, and assign more difficult seatwork—all because they can watch everyone's progress more carefully and provide individual or group help when needed.

BUSINESSLIKE APPROACH
AND ACADEMIC ORIENTATION

It is also logical that increased academic engagement, increased opportunities for learning, active teaching, and maintaining a brisk pace demand an academic orientation and a businesslike attitude in the classroom. We have repeatedly stressed the importance of an academic *school* atmosphere, which presupposes an academic *classroom* atmosphere. Effective teachers do, in fact, view classrooms as learning environments and invest most of their class time in academic activities (Brophy & Evertson, 1976). They enjoy working with students but interact with them mainly within a student–teacher relationship.

Brophy and Evertson (1976) described two interesting types of teachers who tend to stimulate the lowest levels of student achievement. The first type included teachers with a too-strong affective orientation. These teachers were more concerned with personal relationships and other affective objectives than with cognitive (basic skills) objectives. The second type, which fortunately was not common, included bitter, disillusioned teachers who were authoritative and discipline-oriented and disliked students. A strong academic orientation, with its intrinsic commitment to successful teaching, was not the style of either of these teacher types.

TEACHER EXPECTATIONS

Teacher expectations are the inferences teachers make about the likely achievement of students and the types of assignments they need (Good & Weinstein, 1986). As we have seen, the notion of high expectations for student achievement is on every list of characteristics of effective schools and effective principals. Teachers who stimulate high achievement expect their students to master the material; consequently, they allocate most class time to instruction and they keep engagement rates high.

The problem is that some teachers behave differently toward students they believe to be of low ability, thereby depressing achievement both directly and indirectly. There is a *direct* effect in that teachers with low expectations are likely to teach less and provide less opportunity for practice and learning, thus lowering academic engagement rates. These teachers also will communicate their low expectations to students, leading to the *indirect* effect of lower student self-expectations and not trying, which again reduces academic engagement. Because these teachers get the poor achievement they expect, the phenomenon has been dubbed the *self-fulfilling prophecy* or the *Pygmalian* effect (e.g., Rosenthal, 1974).

The Brophy and Good (1970, 1974) and Good and Weinstein (1986) model of teacher expectations includes the following five steps:

1. The teacher expects specific behavior and achievement from particular students.

2. Because of these various expectations, the teacher behaves differently toward various students.

3. This differential treatment tells students what behavior and achievement the teacher expects from them, thus affecting their self-concepts, achievement motivation, and aspirations.

4. If such treatment is consistent over time, and if students do not change it in some way, it will shape their achievement and behavior. High-expectation students will be led to achieve at high levels, while low-expectation students will decline.

5. Over time, students' achievement and behavior will conform more and more closely to the performance originally expected of them.

Causes of Lower Expectations

Teacher expectations may be influenced by SES level, race, test scores, comments from other teachers (lounge talk), type of school (suburban, rural, inner-city), student appearance (expensive, cheap, out-of-style clothes), any nonstandard English language patterns, neatness (poor handwriting, disorganization), generalizing from poor behavior, generalizing from a weakness in one area, tracking and grouping patterns, and even seating position—with lower expectations for students seated on the sides and in the back of classrooms (Good & Weinstein, 1986).

Results of Lower Expectations

Many teachers differ sharply in their interactions with students they perceive to be of low ability in contrast with those they perceive as having higher ability. Specifically, a teacher with low expectations of certain students is likely to interact with these students less often, for example, by calling on them less often to answer questions. The teacher also is likely to wait less time for them to answer questions; allow less time for them to correct mistakes before intervening; generally demand less from them; and interact with them more privately. The teacher is likely to give them more directions and offer them fewer choices (Good & Weinstein, 1986).

In terms of feedback and reinforcement, the teacher is likely to give low-expectancy students the answers or else call on someone else, rather than try to improve their responses with cues or additional opportunities to respond. Such a teacher also might reward inappropriate behavior or incorrect responses, criticize these students more often for failure, and yet praise them less often for successes. Informative feedback to their questions is generally briefer and of lower quality than feedback to high-expectancy students.

A teacher with low expectations of some students is likely to pay less attention to them than to their high-expectancy peers and to interact with them in negative ways. For example, the teacher might seat them further away and show less friendliness toward them, including less smiling, eye contact, hugs, or other indicators of attention, responsiveness, and support. (This reduced friendliness may be more true in high school than in elementary school.) The teacher also is less likely to give these students the benefit of the doubt in borderline grading cases. Some teachers, however, do the opposite—giving them higher grades than the teachers think they really deserve.

In teaching reading, teachers have been found to give briefer reading assignments to low-expectancy students and use less time for discussions of stories. They also tend to interrupt these students more often when they make reading mistakes. In their reading instruction they emphasize decoding words rather than understanding language, and they ask fewer high-level comprehension questions.

Overall, these teacher behaviors not only retard learning directly, they also communicate their low expectations to the students (Brophy & Good, 1974; Good & Weinstein, 1986). Alloway (1984) recorded some disturbingly direct expectancy-loaded comments such as the following:

> "You children are slower, so please get on with your work now."

> "I'll be over to help you slow ones in a minute. This group can go on by itself."

> "The blue group will find this hard."

> "Hurry up, Robyn. Even you can get this right."

Such teacher behaviors and comments toward low-expectancy students naturally depress student motivation and reduce teaching effectiveness.

Improving Expectations

Good and Weinstein (1986) and Dweck and Elliot (1983) noted that teachers' conceptions of intelligence influence their expectations and classroom behavior. Specifically, teachers who see intelligence as *fixed and stable* are more likely to acquire performance expectations that also are fixed. They are not likely to make an extra effort to raise students' performance above the expected level. In contrast, teachers who assume intelligence to be a *modifiable repertoire of skills and knowledge* will not form fixed expectations and are likely to communicate to students that (a) individual differences in rates and modes of learning are normal and (b) each student has the ability to improve regardless of current status.

A reasonable approach is to assume a modifiable view of intelligence, communicate rigorous expectations to all students, and teach in accord with the expectation that all students are capable of grade-level performance or above.

Because of their low expectations, many teachers blame students for poor achievement and interpret failure as a need to provide *less* challenge and *fewer* opportunities for learning. A more productive view is to interpret poor performance as a need for *more* instruction, *more* clarification, and *more* opportunities for learning (Good, 1983; Good & Weinstein, 1986).

Finally, a seemingly self-evident strategy for overcoming the self-fulfilling prophecy is for teachers to become aware of the behaviors they have that transmit low expectations, to be aware of the effects of these communicated expectations, and to change accordingly. Teachers also should look past linguistic deficiencies, student appearance, school location, average school SES level, and similar factors and refuse to adopt the self-fulfilling attitude that "this kid can't learn."

CLASSROOM MANAGEMENT

It is not necessary to reiterate the entire contents of Chapter 4. However, a good point to remember is that classroom management and good instructional strategies are closely interwoven. Good management procedures primarily reduce opportunities for distractions, boredom, and disruptions and thus increase academic engagement and opportunity for learning.

Inset 5-1 summarizes most of the ideas and principles in the teacher training study conducted by Anderson, Evertson, and

INSET 5-1

Principles of Effective Teaching

Using an experimental approach, Anderson, Evertson, and Brophy (1979, 1982) increased the effectiveness of first-grade reading teachers by helping them master some research-based principles derived from the literature on teaching effectiveness. The general principles included the following:

1. Maintaining active engagement and sustained focus on the content, largely through good organization and management.
2. Using tasks and questions that are sufficiently clear and easy that a brisk pace may be maintained, yet with high success rates.
3. Providing frequent opportunities for reading and responding to questions (followed by clear feedback about correctness).
4. Mastering skills to an overlearning level.
5. Closely monitoring progress and providing whatever instruction is required for learning.

Turning to specific recommendations (which are condensed from an even lengthier list), Anderson, Evertson, and Brophy (1982) recommended the following:

In the area of *programming for continuous progress,* effective teachers

1. Successfully manage both the teacher-led small group and students who are working independently.
2. Provide independent workers with appropriate assignments, rules, and routines to follow when help is needed.
3. Provide independent workers with activity options for when they finish their work.
4. Move through the curriculum and specific activities at a brisk pace, using small steps and a high success rate designed to produce continuous progress with relative ease.

(continued)

5. Ask questions that may be answered correctly about 80% of the time. (Lower rates may be expected with new material. Review responses should be almost 100% correct.)

6. Continue practice and review until correct responding is smooth and rapid.

In the area of *group organization,* effective teachers

7. Arrange small-group seating so that the rest of the class also can be monitored.

8. Teach students to move quickly into the small group, bring needed materials, and make other transitions between activities smoothly and quickly.

9. Have materials ready in advance so that the small-group lessons can begin quickly.

10. Begin lessons with an overview to establish the proper mental set and help students anticipate what will be learned.

11. Make certain all students understand what to do and how to do it before releasing them for independent work.

To ensure *participation by all students,* successful teachers

12. Have students take turns in reading or responding so that all have opportunities to participate. (Note: Although this recommendation contradicts Kounin's group-alerting principle described in Chapter 4, Anderson and colleagues argued that taking turns improves management by reducing students' handwaving and other attempts to get the teacher to call on them.)

13. Minimize call-outs. (Students must learn to wait their turn and respect the turns of others. However, calling out sometimes may be encouraged in order to pick up the pace or stimulate interest, for example, with low achievers or students who typically do not volunteer their responses.)

14. Monitor the progress of everyone in the small group with questioning (each student must receive feedback and achieve mastery.)

In the area of *teacher questions and student answers,* effective teachers

15. Concentrate most questions on academic content rather than personal experiences.

16. Wait for an answer if a student is thinking and may be able to respond. (The teacher should stop waiting if the student seems confused or might become embarrassed or if the rest of the group might lose attention.)

17. Provide help with responses by simplifying or rephrasing the question or by giving clues when needed.

18. Answer the question themselves or call on another student when a student cannot respond. (Attention should be focused on the answer, not the student's failure.)

19. Acknowledge that the answer is correct with a brief "correct" or "right," unless the correctness is obvious, as during fast-paced reviewing.

20. Use follow-up questions to help students integrate relevant information when needed. (Questioning also may be extended to help students see logical conclusions.)

21. Use feedback that explains the steps or method necessary for reaching the answer if an answer requires problem solving or reasoning. (Even if the answer is correct, other students might need help to understand why the answer was correct.)

Regarding the use of *praise and criticism,* effective teachers

22. Specify what is being praised—the academic correctness of the response—unless it is obvious to the student and the rest of the group.

23. Always provide corrective feedback for incorrect responses, but focus the correction on the academic content. They do not criticize.

24. Specify the behavior that is being criticized and desirable alternative behavior if criticism should be necessary (e.g., for a behavior problem).

Brophy (1979, 1982). This project was designed to increase the effectiveness of first-grade reading teachers. Many of the principles derived from it relate directly to increasing engagement via good management, along with ideas for increasing clarity, eliciting and reacting to student responses, and monitoring student progress and mastery.

ORGANIZING AND STRUCTURING LEARNING

Organizing and structuring teaching activities to improve learning is not independent of maintaining high academic engagement. However, the focus is more strongly on procedures that make the learning process clearer and more rewarding for students and more efficient for everyone. Better use is made of the engaged time, and teaching is more effective.

ORIENTING STUDENTS, REVIEWING, AND PRESENTING OBJECTIVES

Students must be oriented to learn new material. Such an orientation often includes a review of homework, a review of previous material and skills, an explanation of the purposes and objectives of the new material, and a statement of the relationship of the current lesson to previous material. Ausubel (1978) would say that such orienting comments serve as *advance organizers* that help make the new material more meaningful, easier to relate to what students already know, and therefore more learnable.

There has been much attention in the literature on teaching effectiveness to the importance of opening reviews (Berliner, 1986a; Good, Grouws, & Ebmeier, 1983; Rosenshine, 1986). For example, Rosenshine stressed that at the outset of a lesson effective teachers will spend approximately 5 to 8 minutes reviewing previous material and relevant prior knowledge, making sure that all students are ready for the current lesson and a new homework assignment. The daily review is particularly critical for teaching material of a cumulative nature, material such as mathematics, reading, foreign languages, or computer skills that will be necessary for subsequent learning.

The teacher can review homework assignments, ask about items that were particularly difficult, provide extra instruction and practice with facts and skills that need reteaching, and then review concepts and skills needed for today's lesson and tomorrow's homework. Berliner (1986a) confirmed that opening homework reviews are indeed critical, although, he said, we must clarify more precisely when they are needed and when they are not. Berliner also noted the keen ability of some effective teachers to use the opening homework review to inform "themselves about the difficulty of the assignment, identify students who are not prepared, are having trouble, or who are breezing through and could easily become bored."

Not only daily reviews, but weekly and monthly reviews help supply the repetition, elaboration, and overlearning that aid students in remembering and using the material at a more automatic and effortless level.

In presenting new lessons, teachers should orient students to the new material by explaining lesson purposes and objectives and how the material will be useful (Hunter, 1984), perhaps using an outline or overview. Objectives, outlines, and overviews help focus students' attention, reduce the complexity of the presentation, and help students relate the new material to previous knowledge and skills. The objectives, outline, or overview also help the teacher stay on target. They may be posted or handed out and referred to whenever necessary to help maintain focus.

Opening reviews and introduction of new material comprise a good portion of Rosenshine's (1986) six principles of explicit teaching (see Inset 5-2).

DEVELOPING EFFICIENT ROUTINES: AUTOMATION AND PATTERN RECOGNITION

A series of pioneering studies by Leinhardt (1985) and Leinhardt and Greeno (1986) compared the classroom performance of expert teachers with that of novice student teachers. A major conclusion was that the classroom routines of expert teachers become automated and sophisticated. Goals for a lesson, time constraints, and the subject matter itself become smoothly blended into efficient teacher activities. For example, with opening homework reviews the expert teachers required about one-third less time than the novices. Moreover, expert teachers become extremely percep-

INSET 5–2

Six Principles of Explicit Teaching

Barak Rosenshine's research and reviews related to effective teachers led to a formulation in 1986 of six principles for teaching knowledge and skills in any well-structured subject area, for example, mathematics, reading, English grammar, science, social studies, and foreign language vocabulary and grammar.

According to Rosenshine, all teachers use some of the six principles some of the time. However, effective teachers use all of them most of the time and implement them consistently and systematically. In practice, teachers must use a lot of art, creativity, and thoughtfulness in order to apply these ideas effectively with different students and different subject areas.

1. *Providing daily review.* At the outset of the lesson, effective teachers will review concepts and skills to make sure that all students are ready for new material and for the homework assignment. The review may include discussing the homework assignment, asking about particularly difficult aspects of the homework, and providing extra practice on facts and skills that require reteaching.

2. *Presenting new material.* A central principle of effective instruction is that successful teachers spend more time presenting new material and guiding instruction than do less effective ones. The first step in presenting new material is to state lesson goals, perhaps in the form of an outline or short list of behavioral objectives in order to focus learners' attention and reduce the complexity of the presentation. Effective teachers give more explanations and examples, check for student understanding, and provide sufficient instruction to ensure that students are thoroughly ready for independent practice in seatwork. As Rosenshine noted, some important points are to teach in small steps, use clear language, give step-by-step directions, model the behavior by going through the directions, and organize the material so that each point is mastered before proceeding to the next.

3. *Conducting guided practice.* Guided practice is the supervision of students' initial practice on a skill. After guided

practice, students should be able to perform the steps in a skill correctly, but not yet at a fully automated and fluent level.

Guided practice can involve working problems or responding to teacher questions. Questions usually are of two types, either asking for specific answers or asking for explanations of processes ("How is this done?" "Why is this the correct answer?"). Effective teachers ask a greater number of questions (Stallings & Kaskowitz, 1974) and they ask more process questions (Evertson, Anderson, Anderson, & Brophy, 1980) than do ineffective teachers. Answers at this stage should be correct about 70 to 80% of the time, which represents a good combination of success and appropriate challenge.

Students also can identify which concept class specific examples belong in, as when teaching parts of speech, or they can create their own examples. Some can work at the chalkboard, others at their seats. Still other guided practice strategies include having students tell their answer to a classmate, write an answer on a small chalkboard that is held up for the teacher to see, raise a thumb if they know an answer, or raise a finger if they agree with another's answer. Such procedures keep academic engagement high and help the teacher monitor which students are responding correctly.

4. *Providing feedback and correctives.* If students answer questions with confidence, a short "fine" or "very good" can be followed with another question. However, if a correct answer shows hesitancy or lack of confidence, the teacher can provide process feedback. With this procedure the teacher would say "Yes, that's right because . . ." and then re-explain the procedures necessary to find the right answer.

Errors should be corrected immediately, before they become habitual. A teacher can simplify a question, provide hints, or reteach the material.

5. *Assigning independent practice.* Independent practice is intended to improve the step-by-step, correct-but-hesitant skills to a fluent and automatic level. Independent practice is a continuation of guided practice, covering the same material and skills but now with little or no supervision, as in homework or independent seatwork. If the work is difficult, however, the initial independent practice would be seatwork that is monitored closely.

One effective seatwork strategy is having students help each other. Students usually achieve at higher levels when they work cooperatively. The benefits derive both from having to explain

(continued)

the material to someone else and from having someone other than the teacher explain the concepts.

6. *Providing weekly and monthly review.* In addition to daily reviews, weekly and monthly reviews provide further beneficial practice, practice associated with high achievement. Rosenshine recommended a review of the previous week's accomplishments every Monday, with a monthly review every fourth Monday.

---

tive in their ability to detect meaningful patterns in student responses and behavior. The experts in the studies quickly picked up information about who was absent, who did or did not complete the homework, and who was going to need special help with the next material. They moved at a brisk pace, used clear start and stop signals, never lost control of the lesson, and by teaching clearly and controlling difficulty levels elicited mostly correct answers throughout the activity.

Novice teachers usually did the reverse. They were more likely to have problems taking attendance and determining who did not complete the homework, and they sometimes asked ambiguous questions that made it impossible to determine the difficulty of the homework. Novices generally were unsure of their roles and sometimes lost control of the pace. According to Calderhead (1983), student teachers lack the experience and conceptual structures that permit them to make sense of classroom life.

Expert teachers' sophisticated and automated knowledge of teaching was nicely illustrated in a simple demonstration by Leinhardt and Greeno (1986). Experts and novices were asked to categorize 40 randomly selected fourth-grade mathematics problems and explain their categorizations. Experts used about 10 categories, based on the anticipated difficulty of teaching the problems. Novices used many more categories, based on obvious problem differences.

Expert teachers begin their daily review with well-practiced routines coupled with perceptive visual scanning of the class. Brooks and Hawke (1985) recommended the following routine for opening a junior high class period:

Develop a routine opening that features visual scanning, a quick call to order in a businesslike tone of voice, a method of roll taking that is time efficient, and an opening verbal sequence that includes behavioral and academic expectations. Anticipate areas of confusion in explanations, and call for questions before signaling the beginning of the first activity. Threats to an efficient opening appear to include: The absence of an effective day-to-day behavior routine, a slower call to order in a non-businesslike tone of voice, the absence of visual scanning, a procedure for taking roll that is time consuming, the inability to anticipate confusion, and the absence of advanced organization.

It can take up to 5 years of teaching experience to develop efficient strategies for coping with some problems, according to Huberman (1985). Some of his examples of difficult problems included disciplining students, effectively teaching both slow and fast students, maintaining the interest of unmotivated students, finding a variety of material that students enjoy working with, and establishing a satisfactory set of classroom requirements.

Huberman's comments suggest that there is little substitute for experience. However, there also is no doubt that a beginning teacher who is well informed about effective schools and effective teaching will more quickly develop successful teaching and management routines and make sense of classroom patterns.

INCREASING CLARITY

There are many ways to increase clarity and thus improve student understanding and achievement. In addition to using reviews, objectives, outlines, and overviews, effective teachers give clear verbal and written directions. They repeat key points and instructions and call attention to main ideas. They give additional explanations and examples whenever necessary. They structure and sequence the material to maximize clarity, and they emphasize transition points between lesson parts. They check for understanding by asking clear questions and making sure that all students have a chance to respond, including the quieter ones. They reduce confusion by avoiding digressions and irrelevant content (or the addition of relevant content at the wrong time), that is, Kounin's (1977) flip-flops and dangles (Chapter 4). They also review the main ideas and subparts at the end of the lesson.

All of these techniques help structure, clarify, and reinforce the learning task. They help students synthesize information into integrated wholes, with an understanding of the relationships among parts. These techniques are used by effective teachers, and all are positively related to student achievement (Brophy & Good, 1985).

Clarity—as contrasted with vagueness—has received some analytic research attention (e.g., Smith & Land, 1981). One study compared two passages that were identical except that so-called *vagueness terms* were added. The following paragraph with vagueness terms in roman type will explain why the group without the terms retained more:

> *This mathematics lesson* might *enable you to understand a* little more *about* some things *we* usually *call number patterns.* Maybe *before we get to* probably *the main idea of the lesson, you should review* a few *prerequisite concepts.* Actually, *the first concept you need to review is positive integers.* As you know, *a positive integer is any whole number greater than zero.*

This is a good example of how more can be less. Hiller, Fisher, and Kaess (1969) specifically mentioned the vagueness inherent in such ambiguous and indeterminate terms as *pretty much, some, a few, not many, not very, almost, could be, sometimes, somewhere,* and *often.*

Another bad habit that reduces clarity is the use of so-called verbal mazes, which include false starts, backtracks, redundancies, and generally tangled words. From Smith and Land (1981):

> *This mathematics lesson will* enab . . . *will get you to understand* number, *uh, number patterns. Before we get to* the main idea of the, *main idea of the lesson, you need to review* four conc . . . *four prerequisite concepts. The first* idea, I mean, uh, *concept you need to review is positive integers. A positive* number . . . *integer is any whole* integer, uh, *number greater than zero.*

One study actually investigated the effects of saying "uh" too much, finding that, indeed, the use of "uh" slightly depressed achievement (Smith, 1977). Another study created high-clarity and low-clarity teaching conditions. In the low-clarity condition, teachers' presentations were replete with vagueness terms, mazes, superfluous content, and plenty of "uh's." The high-clarity condition included none of these, but did include an emphasis on key aspects of the content to be learned and clear signaling of transitions between lesson parts. To no one's surprise, the clear lessons produced better learning (Land, 1979).

Brophy and Good (1985) concluded that "in general, clarity of presentation is one of the more consistent correlates of achievement." Walberg (1985) noted that of seven published studies of the effects of clarity, all seven—100%—showed a benefit for learning and achievement.

ENSURING HIGH SUCCESS RATES

A traditional assumption in teaching has been that students require challenging learning tasks, tasks of intermediate difficulty. This idea has been disproved. Research shows that students need and enjoy very high success rates, which come only from tasks at an appropriate difficulty level that are clearly taught and readily comprehended. For example, Brophy and Evertson (1974a, 1974b, 1976) found that high-SES elementary children learned best when the teachers' questions elicited about 70% correct responses, while low-SES pupils learned best with about 80% correct answers to questions. They concluded that learning proceeds best when the material is somewhat new or challenging, yet relatively easy for children to understand and integrate with existing knowledge and skills. Another study concluded that for younger students and less able students, almost errorless performance during learning produces better achievement and greater satisfaction (Marliave & Filby, 1986).

Note that seatwork and homework assignments, which require independent effort, should elicit close to 100% correct responding. Student responses should be rapid, smooth, and almost always correct (Berliner, 1984). Brophy (1983) pointed out that homework and seat assignments demand the application of skills and knowledge that must be mastered to the point of overlearning if they are to be retained and applied to still more complex material. High success rates in seatwork and homework are achieved both by selecting tasks at an appropriate difficulty level and by explaining them clearly and thoroughly before work begins.

The true value of seatwork, the way it often is used, has been questioned in recent years. Berliner (1986b), in an article entitled

"When Kids Do Seatwork, What Do They Do?" argued that seatwork should be more than a task "to finish as quickly as possible." He cited Anderson's research on reading instruction with high- and low-achieving first-grade children in which she found that students usually did not understand the reasons for the seatwork tasks, the goals of the instruction, or the ways any of the skills they were learning in seatwork fit together. When she examined what students actually were doing in their seatwork, she found that 51% of the assignments only required students to mark one out of a limited number of options. A large proportion of tasks required copying, and neatness and accurate reproduction were the main criteria. Of the tasks presented, 35% required single associations between letters, sounds, and words or pictures, and 40% required comprehension of single sentences. Just 9% of all assignments required students to understand two or more related sentences in order to answer a question; that is, to read with comprehension.

Teachers were found to check seatwork quickly, often giving credit for assignments that individual students had never completed. Most low-achieving students had trouble with their seatwork, yet their short-term strategy of "getting the work done quickly" often fooled the teacher into thinking they were learning more than they were.

In short, Anderson concluded that students were learning little or nothing when they did all of that seatwork, other than learning to finish it as quickly as possible. One child, Randy, cried with delight, "It's done!" He explained that he did not like long assignments because "it takes so long I can't play." Richard stated, "I don't know what it means, but I did it!" Beth and her neighbor were in a race to see who would finish first. At the end of each sentence, Beth raised her hands in silent cheer for her speed.

Anderson's study suggests that little knowledge may be gained from seatwork, as evidenced, for example, by children who consistently made the same mistakes when reading after completing the related seatwork correctly. However, seatwork should not be abandoned. Berliner (1986b) concluded that Anderson's study shows a strong need for careful selection, presentation, explanation, monitoring, and evaluation of seatwork.

As a general tendency, according to Brophy (1983), teachers are much more likely to assign tasks that are too difficult than ones that are too easy. One study showed that during a full 14% of the time they were observed, teachers gave assignments that, incredibly enough, elicited 100% *incorrect* responses. Students experienced total failure during these periods. Berliner (1984) has shown that high error rates correlate negatively with achievement, which is hardly surprising.

Another study showed that fourth-grade teachers identified as effective tried not to ask mathematics questions that would produce either incorrect answers or no answers at all (Good, Grouws, & Beckerman, 1978). These teachers instructed more clearly, interweaving explanations with questions. Less clear teachers, whose students achieved at lower levels, spent more time correcting unsatisfactory responses and attempting to clarify the assignments.

One basic reason why success levels can be low is that at the beginning of the year or semester teachers rarely find out exactly where students are in a particular subject. This is not a great problem at the elementary school level because students move from grade to grade as a group and curriculum planners, teachers, and administrators monitor subject continuity through the grades. In the middle school and high school, however, variations in students' entry levels of mastery are a significant problem. Secondary school teachers have little information about individual students' backgrounds. Pretesting, if only as an informal discussion, is essential in order to match goals, objectives, and methods to students' current knowledge and skills. An inappropriate curriculum will cause low success levels—the failure, frustration, and poor self-esteem that lead high school students to drop out. The best effective-teaching plans will be wasted if they are aimed at the wrong entering level of student achievement.

We have three final comments on maintaining appropriate success levels. First, when monitoring comprehension and success rates during question-and-answer recitations, teachers should not forget that questions should be directed to all students, not just the ones whose hands are raised or who sit in the front and center of the class. Second, if individualized mastery learning strategies are used, a good procedural rule to follow is that students should score at least 90% correct on a diagnostic test before proceeding to the next unit. Corrective feedback, reteaching, and remedial assignments are used when students do not perform successfully on their first effort. Third, in addition to continually monitoring success rates during questioning, seatwork, and homework, effective teachers watch grade-book records of daily assignments and unit tests to detect individual or class trends in mastery.

Are high success rates important? A high success rate indicates that students are comprehending and mastering the information and skills. As Berliner (1984) put it, "Success rate . . . appears to be another powerful variable with known effects on achievement. Like other such classroom variables, it needs to be monitored, evaluated, and often modified." Berliner included high success rates in his concept of academic learning time, described earlier in this chapter as time students spend engaged in academic tasks related to test content that are performed with high rates of success (see Figure 5-1). Squires, Huitt, and Segars (1983) built a model for school and classroom effectiveness around just three crucial variables: high academic involvement (engagement), high amounts of content coverage, and high student success rates on daily assignments.

In Inset 5-3, Madeline Hunter makes suggestions regarding the art and science of teaching that should improve students' success rates and therefore their academic achievement.

MONITORING STUDENT PROGRESS

The topic of monitoring student progress has several interrelated meanings, and it runs through many of the topics already discussed. For example, academic engagement rates in seatwork are much higher when the teacher moves rapidly about, monitoring the work; that is, checking to see whether students are doing things correctly. When unwatched, or unmonitored, student engagement rates in seatwork and small-group work will decline (Berliner, 1984). We just described how success rates—which are a function of teaching clarity, appropriate difficulty levels, and student comprehension—also are monitored in teacher questioning, seatwork, homework, and records of daily assignments and unit tests. Monitoring of progress also takes place in daily interactions, as when teachers answer student questions.

In effective schools monitoring of student progress takes place at all levels. Effective teachers monitor minute-to-minute comprehension, success, and engagement rates, along with the longer term achievement records of every student. Effective principals monitor achievement scores for individual students, classes, and grade levels. Improvement-minded superintendents also monitor average achievement scores for their classes and schools, comparing them with schools in other districts and with national averages.

Whatever level or form monitoring student progress takes, effective administrators and teachers use the achievement information as the basis for modifications of teaching and/or school-wide improvement plans.

INSET 5–3

Madeline Hunter

The ideas of Madeline Hunter (1984, 1985) are having such an impact on teaching theory and practice that the phrase "We've been Hunterized" has become a standard quip. Agreeing with Nathan Gage, Hunter has conceded that teaching requires both art and science. Hunter, however, has emphasized the scientific side of the scale, drawing on cause–effect relationships derived mainly from psychology; that is, she employs "psychological principles that contribute to the speed and effectiveness with which each student acquires new learnings. . . ." Viewing the teacher as a continual decision maker, Hunter has identified the professional decisions teachers must make and supplied research-based cause–effect relationships to guide those decisions. The artistry, according to Hunter, "can exist in planning, in teaching, and in the evaluation of teaching performance."

Hunter's goal has been to help teachers know what to consider before deciding what to do, basing their decisions on sound theory. For example, she has recommended task-analyzing district objectives in order to decide which specific teaching and learning activities that "will be taught tomorrow morning" will lead to mastering those larger objectives. She also has recommended that teachers closely analyze students' learning activities—reading, listening, observing, discussing, experimenting, recording, and so forth. Is what they do appropriate to what is to be learned? Is what a particular student is doing "working" for that student?

Other psychological principles relate to increasing intrinsic motivation, using reinforcers to enhance self-concepts, and relating new learning to a student's life to make the learning more meaningful and useful. Effectively using these and other principles involves "the greatest artistry in teaching," according to Hunter (1984).

Hunter has incorporated psychological principles in each of seven steps of an instructional model that closely resembles Rosenshine's six principles of explicit teaching presented in Inset 5-2:

1. *Anticipatory set* involves helping students focus on what will be learned.

(continued)

2. *Objective and purpose* are explaining to students what will be learned and how it will be useful.

3. *Input* is the knowledge and skills derived from the task analysis, which may be presented by a variety of teaching and learning activities.

4. *Modeling* is helping students view in a concrete way the process or product they are expected to acquire or produce.

5. *Checking for understanding.* An often-cited Hunter device is having students raise a finger if they understand a direction or if they agree with another student's answer.

6. *Guided practice* is practicing the new knowledge or skill under direct teacher supervision.

7. *Independent practice* "is assigned only after the teacher is reasonably sure that students will not make serious errors."

"Competence," according to Hunter, "is knowing what we're doing, why it works, and doing it on purpose."

IMPORTANCE OF WAIT TIME

Wait time is defined as "the duration of the pause after a teacher (or student) utterance" (Tobin, 1987). The fact is, teachers usually rush. Explanations of the beneficial effects of longer wait times usually are based on information-processing concepts. Basically, a longer wait time gives students a better opportunity to process the information, that is, perceive and interpret the message, understand the cognitive skills and processes required, use the skills or processes to create or manipulate information, and then encode (store) the information in a retrievable form. Longer wait times logically are needed for processing more complex verbal messages.

Earlier in this chapter we noted that moving at a brisk pace increases academic engagement and content coverage and therefore leads to higher achievement. However, Brophy and Good

(1985) have suggested that rapid pacing may be most effective in the early grades because it maintains momentum (and attention) and seems to suit the type of learning that takes place in these grades. At higher grade levels, teachers make longer presentations on more abstract or complex content. Therefore, a slower pace (longer wait time) often is necessary to allow new concepts to be absorbed.

Unless there has been a chance for processing to occur, the auditory input is likely to fade from the storage system and be lost. Try this demonstration. Open this book to any other page, read one sentence, then stop for a moment. The content of the sentence will remain in your short-term memory (sometimes called an "echo box") for a while. Then turn to another page. Read a sentence, then quickly read a few more randomly selected sentences on randomly selected pages. This time the sentence probably is lost from memory due to interference from reading the other sentences. A longer teacher wait time reduces interference, permits processing, and, according to recent research, leads to higher achievement (Tobin, 1987).

As an example of wait times that are too fast, Shrum (1985) reported that in high school Spanish and French classes, after posing a question, teachers waited an average of just 1.9 seconds before continuing. After students answered, teachers waited an average of just 0.6 seconds before responding. Interestingly, the teachers' wait times were longer when questions were posed to high- and low-ability students, compared with students of average ability. Other studies have shown that wait times are longer for more complex questions, for example, questions requiring divergent thinking, analysis, synthesis, or evaluation (Boeck & Hillenmeyer, 1973; Jones, 1980).

There has been much research focused on wait time. The recent review by Tobin (1987) included 18 research studies with the phrase *wait time* in their titles, plus six more that included *lapse time, think time, pauses, pausing,* and *time.* Tobin concluded:

> *When average wait time is greater than a threshold value of 3 seconds, changes in teacher and student discourse were observed and higher cognitive level achievement was obtained in elementary, middle, and high school science. Achievement increases were also reported in middle school mathematics. Wait time appears to facilitate higher cognitive level learning by providing teachers and students with additional time to think. . . . Teachers should consciously manage the duration of pauses after solicitations and pro-*

vide regular intervals of silence during explanations. . . .
Pauses following student discourse are also of potential
importance.

In a series of classic studies, Rowe (1974a, 1974b, 1974c; see also Swift & Gooding, 1983) concluded that wait times in classes throughout the United States were less than 3 seconds and usually less than 1 second. In his research, wait times after teacher comments or questions (Wait Time I) and after student responses (Wait Time II) were manipulated to be between 3 and 5 seconds. With these longer wait times, Rowe found that teachers asked fewer but more appropriate questions and generally demonstrated greater response flexibility. The number of students failing to respond decreased. Teachers also developed higher expectations for students previously rated as slow learners, because the longer wait times led to an increase in responses from these students.

With increases in Wait Time II, the period after student responses, Rowe found that the quality and quantity of student responses improved. Students increased the length of their responses, number of unsolicited but appropriate responses, and number of responses rated as speculative. Further, the number of interferences supported by evidence increased, which showed greater understanding, attentiveness, involvement, and thoughtfulness.

More recent research has supported these findings. For example, DeTure and Miller (1985) found that when teachers used longer wait times they asked fewer questions. However, while they asked fewer memory-level questions, they asked more creativity-stimulating questions. There also was a general reduction in student confusion with the longer wait times. Swift and Gooding (1983) similarly recorded fewer memory questions and more evaluation questions when longer wait times were imposed. Anderson (1978) reported that with longer teacher wait times students perceived physics content to be less difficult. Other conclusions tied to longer wait times included increased student discourse and fewer failures to respond; increases in the complexity and cognitive level of student responses; more confidence and esprit de corps; fewer student interruptions; higher engagement rates; and higher achievement (e.g., Riley, 1986; Tobin, 1986, 1987; Tobin & Capie, 1982).

Apparently, many teachers have difficulty adjusting to wait times of 3 seconds or longer, which has led to the development of strategies for helping teachers learn to use longer wait times. According to Tobin (1987), analyzing wait time patterns and providing feedback to teachers seems to be the most effective training strategy. According to Morine-Dershimer and Beyerback (1987), however, learning to increase wait time is not difficult at all: "Try counting to 3."

OTHER CHARACTERISTICS OF EFFECTIVE TEACHERS AND TEACHING

There are many other teacher characteristics and teaching patterns that correlate with higher student achievement and/or improved school attitudes, that is, with effective teaching. Most relate to improvement of classroom climate, management, and feedback and reinforcement practices; involvement in self-improvement and staff development; and improvement of other teaching practices that increase student engagement and content coverage and improve organization, structuring and clarity, expectations, or student interest and motivation.

Some research-based correlates of teacher effectiveness in the area of *classroom climate* include the following:

- Having strong interpersonal skills, particularly empathy, respect, and genuineness.
- Having good relationships with students.
- Genuinely accepting and caring about students.
- Expressing interest and enthusiasm.
- Creating an atmosphere of cooperation and group cohesiveness.
- Involving students in organizing and planning.
- Listening to students and respecting their right to speak during recitations and discussions.
- Minimizing friction of any sort.

Some *management* strategies of effective teachers include

- Establishing routines for dealing with inattention, interruptions, turn taking, and transitions.

- Asking questions or presenting tasks that require different levels of thinking.

Included in the area of *feedback and reinforcement* are:

- Giving high rates of positive feedback for student responses.
- Providing supportive responses to low-ability students.
- Attempting to improve initially unsatisfactory answers to questions (e.g., with follow-up questions).
- Providing help when needed.

Some *self-renewal* and *staff-development* characteristics include

- Using innovative curricula and teaching methods.
- Continually expanding one's repertoire of teaching methods.
- Using teacher group planning to create alternative teaching methods (elaborated in Chapter 6).

Other research-based suggestions for improving classroom teaching practices include

- Maintaining relevance between teacher behavior and learning objectives.
- Guarding against treating low-achieving pupils differently, for example, by asking them only factual questions, providing them fewer turns to talk, and giving them shorter wait times.
- Managing accountability by inspecting work and displaying products publicly, in addition to assigning grades.
- Enticing students to try difficult tasks by using bonus points.
- Balancing concrete and abstract terminology.
- Using accurate examples.
- Giving definitions, examples, and labels for concepts.
- Using analogies between new material and events that are already familiar to students to increase clarity.

- Asking questions that require students to apply, analyze, synthesize, and evaluate in addition to recalling facts.

- Improving reading ability by encouraging reading in and out of school.

- Telling stories to young children to motivate reading and teach cultural values.

- Having children perform experiments to see science "in action."

- Using physical objects to teach mathematics to young children more effectively.

- Involving parents in children's school work.

Inset 5-4 summarizes findings of the long-term Beginning Teacher Evaluation Study, a major government-supported effort to identify characteristics of effective teachers. Interested readers also should see Brophy and Good (1985), Walberg (1985), and the U.S. Department of Education's (1987) *What Works* booklet.

SUMMARY

Statistical correlations between teacher variables and achievement are low. However, even weak relationships can make important differences. Furthermore, the effects of effective-schooling variables are additive.

Academic engagement is the most important factor contributing to student achievement. Academic learning time (Berliner) is time engaged in activities related to the outcome measure, during which a student experiences a high rate of success. Allocated time, opportunity to learn, and amount of content covered are related to each other, to academic engagement, and to achievement.

Teachers vary dramatically in the amount of time they allocate, for example, to reading or mathematics. However, Stallings confirmed that reading and mathematics scores were related to the amount of class time spent on these subjects. Time spent in nonacademic activities was not correlated with achievement. The amount of content covered (quantity of instruction) was Stallings's strongest correlate of achievement.

INSET 5–4

Beginning Teacher Evaluation Study

In the early 1970s, the Far West Regional Laboratory and the Educational Testing Service, with funding from the National Institute of Education, launched the Beginning Teacher Evaluation Study (BTES). This major exploration of teacher effectiveness focused on identifying specific teacher characteristics and classroom behaviors correlated with student achievement. The following briefly summarizes the extensive findings and recommendations of this series of research studies.

In the area of *organization,* teachers who produce high achievement

1. Emphasize academic, not affective goals. (Note: In the late 1980s the pendulum is swinging away from emphasizing strictly teacher-centered academic goals and back to including student-centered affective goals—good self-concepts, citizenship, academic motivation, independence, etc.)

2. Are well organized.

3. Are knowledgeable about their subject matter.

4. Structure learning experiences well.

5. Are unlikely to fill time with busywork instead of initiating more profitable activities.

6. Give clear task directions before independent seatwork or homework begins.

7. Use aides or other adults to supplement instruction, if available.

In relation to the use of *class time,* these teachers

8. Maximize time devoted to instruction by allocating adequate time and maintaining high engagement rates.

9. Move briskly through the curriculum.

10. Spend most class time actively instructing and monitoring seatwork.

11. Spend minimum classroom time on preparation, procedural matters, or discipline.

12. Ensure that students spend adequate time practicing and applying skills.

13. Keep students attentive to lessons and engaged in their assignments when working alone.

14. Involve all students in recitation and discussion, not just a subgroup (e.g., students who raise their hands and students who sit in front).

Effective teachers establish a pleasant, businesslike, and academic classroom *climate*. They

15. Let students know that they enjoy teaching.

16. Are polite and pleasant yet businesslike.

17. Call students by name and attend carefully to what students say.

18. Elicit student responsibility and cooperation in doing academic work.

19. Involve students in decision making.

20. Receive high ratings by students on cooperation, work engagement, and conviviality of the classroom. There is mutual respect, instead of the conflict found in lower achieving classes.

Classroom *management* practices also are good. Successful teachers

21. Are unlikely to make management errors such as switching abruptly back and forth between instruction and discipline.

22. Do not ignore, belittle, harass, shame, put down, or exclude their students, who in turn are less likely to defy or try to manipulate their teachers.

23. Are consistent in following through on directions and demands.

24. Are unlikely to make illogical, confusing statements.

(continued)

Daily *teaching practices and habits* are good. In this category effective teachers

25. Accurately predict students' difficulty with particular material.

26. Match the difficulty level of content to students' present achievement levels.

27. Make demands on students, encouraging them to work hard and take responsibility for their academic progress.

28. Monitor individual and class progress carefully.

29. Individualize instruction.

30. Adjust readily to unexpected events and emergent instructional opportunities.

31. Are unlikely to call attention to themselves for no apparent reason.

In the process of recitation and *providing feedback,* successful teachers

32. Provide appropriate academic feedback related to correctness of answers and responses.

33. Praise students' successes.

34. Maintain high success rates in responding. (Very high success rates are especially important for younger and slower learning students.)

35. Are likely to ask open-ended questions to help increase understanding.

36. Wait long enough for answers to encourage thinking and volunteering of answers.

Overall, these effective teachers are more committed to instruction, more knowledgeable, and more active and demanding in their teaching than their less effective peers. Class time is used for instruction, and engagement rates are high. Their instruction is paced to students' needs. They show good organization, management, and diagnostic skills and use feedback effectively. Warm personal traits create a positive atmosphere that stimulates student attention and cooperation.

These traits and behaviors unambiguously add up to high achievement, good classroom behavior, and good school attitudes. For further information, see Berliner and Tikunoff (1976, 1977), Berliner, Fisher, Filby, and Marliave (1978), Denham and Lieberman (1980), Fisher and colleagues (1980), McDonald (1976), and McDonald and Elias (1976).

Stallings suggested that teachers can make better use of class time by spending time with groups instead of individuals, directly instructing students, and closely monitoring independent work. The traditional teaching pattern of questions, responses, and feedback was recommended.

Ideas for what *not* to do—teacher behaviors negatively related to achievement—include getting organized during class time instead of teaching, offering students choices of activities, losing time to interruptions, and imposing lengthy seatwork assignments.

According to Stallings, class time should be used by teachers for organizing (15%), interactive instruction (50%), and monitoring (35%). Academic statements should comprise 80% of classroom interactions.

The selection of curriculum content also influences opportunities for learning and content coverage, and therefore achievement. Several recommendations in the effective-schooling literature can aid learning by increasing time allocations, opportunities for learning, and content coverage, for example, establishing and following time-use guidelines.

Effective teachers are active and maintain a brisk pace, thus sustaining interest and allowing good content coverage. Classes and lessons should be started and ended promptly. Development of thinking skills, however, may suffer from a too-brisk pace.

Smaller class size, a businesslike approach, and an academic orientation all improve achievement.

Teacher expectations, influenced by SES, race, test scores, and other teachers' comments, can raise or lower student achievement. Teachers with low expectations may teach students less (direct effect) and lower students' self-expectations (indirect effect).

The Brophy and Good expectation model includes the steps of (1) expecting certain behavior or achievement of particular students, (2) behaving differently toward these students, (3) influencing their self-concepts and achievement motivation, thereby (4) lowering their achievement and resulting in (5) long-term changes in the direction of the (low) expectations.

A teacher should assume that intelligence, as a skill repertoire, is modifiable. Failure indicates a need for *more* instruction, not less.

Classroom management and good teaching strategies are closely related. Organizing and structuring learning is aided by presenting lesson purposes and objectives (advance organizers) and by using daily opening reviews plus weekly and monthly reviews. Expert teachers develop efficient, automated routines and can recognize meaningful behavior patterns.

While Huberman estimated that a period of 5 years is needed to develop efficient teaching and management strategies, information about effective schools and teachers should expedite the process.

Clarity, in the form of giving comprehensible directions; repeating key points; and providing good structuring, sequencing, and review improves understanding and learning. Clarity is reduced by vague terms and verbal mazes.

Maintaining high success rates depends on selecting tasks of appropriate difficulty that are clearly explained and readily comprehended. Younger and less able students require very high success rates. Seatwork and homework should elicit close to 100% correct responses.

Berliner described how Anderson found that seatwork may not be serving its intended purpose, particularly because students race through the work. Seatwork must be carefully selected, explained, and monitored.

Effective teachers instruct more clearly than their less effective peers and try not to ask questions that produce incorrect answers or no answers. Low success rates may be caused by teachers' not knowing their students' entry skills at the beginning of a year or semester.

Recitation questions should be directed to all students. In mastery learning programs, students should score 90% correct before proceding to the next unit. Teachers should monitor both individual and class trends in success levels.

Monitoring means checking the accuracy of seatwork, watching whether students are working, and watching success rates. Also, teachers, principals, and superintendents monitor achievement records.

Wait times (after a teacher question and after a student response) of at least 3 seconds aid learning by allowing information processing. Rowe itemized many benefits of longer wait times.

Other characteristics of effective teachers were classified according to whether they influence classroom climate, management, feedback and reinforcement practices, self-improvement and staff development, and other factors related to, for example, expectations, accountability, motivating learning, increasing clarity, and involving parents.

Chapter Six

Supervision and Coaching by Administrators and Peers

*In schools in which collegial relations prevail . . .
ordinary people, relying on ordinary budgets and
confronted with the ordinary ebb and flow of energy,
goodwill, and creativity, accomplish extraordinary
things.*
—Judith W. Little, "Teachers as Colleagues"

*If teachers are to become partners (rather than
adversaries) in efforts to create improved learning
conditions in our schools, they must be involved in
planning, decision making, and goal setting.*
—Sam Rodriguez and Kathy Johnstone, "Staff Development Through
a Collegial Support Group Model"

*Until we treat teachers as professionals, we cannot
expect them to contribute as professionals to the
school organization.*
—Thomas J. Sergiovanni and F .D. Carver, *The New School Executive:
A Theory of Administration*

As we stressed in Chapter 3, strong instructional leadership by the
principal is one of the most recurrent characteristics of effective
schools. Part of that instructional leadership includes observing
teachers in classrooms and providing feedback regarding ways to
improve their instructional and classroom management skills. This
chapter reviews procedures for classroom observation and
coaching by principals or other administrators in ways that are
positive, constructive, and effective. As we will see, much of the

observation and coaching is based on characteristics of effective schools (Chapter 3) and, especially, characteristics and behaviors of effective teachers (Chapter 5).

It also is true that teachers can and will take responsibility for their own professional development, given administrators who empower them to do so. This chapter also reviews (a) classroom observation and coaching by fellow teachers who are particularly expert regarding effective materials and teaching skills, usually in specialized subject areas, and (b) teacher work groups and teams that solve problems and plan and incorporate innovative curricula and teaching strategies.

Before looking at the details and benefits of current conceptions of administrator supervision, peer observation and coaching, and teacher work groups, let us consider first a few issues related to these topics.

ISOLATION IN TEACHING

Observation and coaching by principals and fellow teachers and the creation of teacher work groups are quite the reverse of traditional conceptions of the teacher's role and duties—conceptions that still exist. The teacher commonly is viewed as a relatively isolated, independent person. Teachers work alone, both out of sight and out of hearing of one another. They plan lessons and materials alone, and they cope with teaching and management problems alone. Fellow teachers are colleagues in name only.

When a new teacher joins a school, under the isolation model his or her introduction to the job is not gradual, as in other careers, but has been described as "abrupt" or "unstaged." New teachers report again and again that they learned on their own by trial and error, or that "it was sink or swim!" (Little, 1987).

A pattern of isolation among both veteran and new teachers remains common in large numbers of schools, although some educational reform programs (e.g., the South Carolina Education Improvement Act; T. Peterson, 1988) specifically include measures for assisting beginning teachers. The isolation of beginning teachers stands in vivid contrast to dynamic and successful interactive models of teaching that stress collective efforts to learn and apply new ideas, methods, and materials. The interactive models center on collaborative planning and problem solving and peer observation and coaching. This approach is leading to high rates of team-work and innovation; strong feelings of accomplishment, competence, enthusiasm, and job satisfaction; improved levels of student achievement and school attitudes (Little, 1987); and better education for at-risk students and students with special needs (Odden, 1988).

ONE–WAY TEACHING

Another traditional conception of teaching that is inconsistent with more dynamic, interactive approaches is the notion of *one-way teaching*. As pictured by the Holmes Group (1986)—a high-level national group concerned with teacher training—the teacher is considered a supposedly bright person and teaching is simplistically reduced to presenting or passing on information. In two modifications, teaching is seen as presenting plus keeping order, or at best planning, presenting, and keeping order. These views assume that the bright and well-educated teacher can develop logical, coherent, and perhaps even interesting presentations that will be delivered and therefore learned by students. The Holmes report warned that "this conception blithely overlooks one of the most critical aspects of quality teaching—the extent to which the lesson is appropriate for the particular students for whom the teacher is responsible and for whom the lessons should be crafted."

The alternate conception, which is consistent with the message of this book, derives from "both time-tested conceptions of teacher qualities and responsibilities, and of recent understandings about role requirements" (Holmes Group, 1986). Namely, according to the Holmes Group, competent teachers should possess a deep understanding of their students, the subjects they teach, and the nature of learning and schooling. They should be empowered by informed administrators to make good, professional judgments and decisions on behalf of their students. They should exemplify the critical thinking and attitudes of inquiry they seek to develop in students. They should not bore, confuse, or demean students but should encourage them to become engaged with important knowledge and skills. Competent teachers identify students' misconceptions and understandings and they question student responses that reflect only superficial learning.

Good teachers also possess the academic and clinical training that enables them to teach students to mastery levels and to deal with complex social relations in the classroom in ways that foster learning and constructive school attitudes (Holmes Group, 1986).

There is more to good teaching than planning, presenting, and keeping order.

SAVING THE BAD APPLE: NEED FOR INSTRUCTIONAL LEADERSHIP

The current teacher shortage has dramatically changed the ways in which administrators view teachers and their approach to school improvement. When teachers were plentiful, an ineffective new teacher, or so-called bad apple, could be identified and replaced relatively easily, assuming tenure had not been granted. Teacher evaluation was dictatorial, and every rock was overturned to locate and eliminate the bad apples. This did not present a problem since there were plenty of willing teachers looking for jobs. Currently, the teacher shortage has caused administrators to look at teachers in a different light. Instead of replacing ineffective teachers, it is more important now to help them become more effective. (Actually, very few of the bad apples were rotten in the first place.)

In *The Incompetent Teacher,* Bridges (1986) noted that when a teacher is performing poorly, administrators tend to blame the teacher for either lack of *ability* ("He/she wasn't very bright," "wasn't on top of the subject matter," "lacked common sense") or lack of *effort* ("He/she was lazy," "was not putting forth the effort," "wasn't motivated, "just putting in the time"). In fact, one very real reason for the poor performance is inadequate supervision—a failure to take corrective action early in a teacher's career. Many principals and assistant principals lack the skills necessary to deal with an incompetent teacher or for that matter to assume many other instructional leadership responsibilities.

It also is true that while a dynamic and proactive principal with vision is critical for creating an effective school, in actuality it is the work force this principal can muster that gets the job done. To be effective, the principal must collaborate with teachers—using them, coaching them, and empowering them to teach what they are experts in. As we mentioned earlier in this book, an effective principal is, in essence, a manager of a group of experts.

Now more than ever the responsibility for improving school effectiveness through instructional leadership lies mainly with the principal. The principal must create a unified atmosphere, one in which staff and students see harmony in the school program, a smooth flow from one content area to another, and all in a climate that values education and achievement. The principal is in the unique leadership position of being visibly appointed as school leader, and he or she should have a broad view of the goals and problems of the school and a vision for improving it.

THE BUSINESS MODEL
APPLIED TO TEACHING

The concept of an academic school climate or culture appeared in all of our earlier discussions of effective schools, effective principals, and effective teachers. Culture can have a powerful effect on work lives, and its nature and importance should be understood by school administrators, teachers, and other staff. An organizational culture, generally, "is a system of informal rules that spells out how people are to behave most of the time" (Deal & Kennedy, 1982). With a guiding set of values—a strong culture—people know what is expected of them; they know what to do and how they should do it; and behavior will be consistent from person to person. According to Deal and Kennedy (1982), with uncertain values people tend to become blameful, cynical, and even less ethical in their professional lives. A strong culture causes people to feel better about what they do and motivates them to work harder toward even greater accomplishments. Holland (1988) referred to a school culture—the shared values, rules, ideology, beliefs, and conceptions—as the *normative glue* that holds the organization together.

Certainly, to be successful a newcomer in a school or corporation must understand the local culture. Any administrator who wishes to succeed must understand both the significance of culture for organizational success and his or her own key role in shaping that culture. An organizational culture may be coherent or fragmented and poorly understood; it may create meaning and guidance or contribute to confusion; it may be strong, rich, and focused or weak and ambiguous.

Recently, increasing attention has been paid to successful corporate cultures and the implications for successful school cultures (e.g., Deal, 1987; Deal & Kennedy, 1982). As Deal and Kennedy noted, "The impact of a strong culture on productivity is amazing. . . . Culture can make them [employees] fast or slow workers, tough or friendly managers, team players or individuals." It is important to note that the most successful administrators and managers are those who, guided by vision, work to shape a shared culture and values. The relevance to education and educational reform should be apparent.

As an example, the *quality circle* concept in business includes the assumption that to be satisfied and motivated employees must take part in company decision making. Excellence is fostered by working with instead of mandating to employees. Opinions are asked for, and employees are empowered to do what they believe in. Is a successful educational organization any different?

Consistent with the educational leadership principles described in Chapter 2, business firms also establish values that aim at better morale and higher productivity. These values define success in terms of concrete standards of achievement: "If you do this, you too will be a success." The so-called strong-culture companies investigated by Deal and Kennedy (1982) all had rich and complex systems of values that were shared by employees. According to these researchers, "Managers in these companies talked about these beliefs openly and without embarrassment."

The following are additional characteristics shared by strong-culture companies:

1. *Heroes.* Just as a school principal can create a reward system to publicly recognize accomplishments of staff and students, an effective corporation will identify heroes whom others can emulate. These people exemplify the culture and values of the corporation and provide role models for employees to follow. Deal and Kennedy noted that "smart companies take a direct hand in choosing people to play these heroic roles, knowing full well that others will try to emulate their behavior." Thomas Edison, for example, is a company hero at General Electric, along with lesser known figures including the inventor of the motor for the electric toothbrush, an export salesman who survived two foreign revolutions, and an international manager who had ghosts exorcised from a Singapore factory.

2. *Rituals and ceremonies.* We have mentioned rituals (e.g., school songs and slogans) that strengthen school spirit and school culture in general. Corporations install similar rituals and ceremonies to provide visible examples of what the company stands for and show employees the kind of behavior that is expected of them ("At Ford, Quality is Number One!").

3. *Cultural network.* The *cultural network* is the informal communication system within a corporation. Tapping into this network will help management understand what is really going on. Further, according to Deal and Kennedy (1982), the network can be manipulated in order to get things done.

Shaping values, making heroes, spelling out rites and rituals, and acknowledging and using the cultural network have created excellent climates at such companies as Apple Computer, General Motors, General Electric, IBM, Walt Disney Productions, and Tandem. The culture, Deal and Kennedy (1982) argued, drives the company. In view of their similar structural organization and morale and productivity problems, it is no wonder that educators are beginning to look to successful corporations for effective principles of leadership and for ways to establish a positive and productive climate.

SECOND-WAVE REFORM

Michaels (1988) and Lieberman (1988) recently summarized the so-called *second-wave reform,* which builds on and extends the effective-schooling movement that is rooted in first-wave reform. The first-wave reform of recent decades "set out to raise standards, increase accountability, lengthen school days and years, and generally raise the rigor of American public education" (Michaels, 1988). The result, said Michaels and the Carnegie Task Force on Teaching as a Profession (1986), was "doing better on the old goals," that is, correcting declining scores in the basics, particularly mathematics and reading.

The agenda of the second wave includes several components, the first of which is *school site management.* This focus on the individual school as the unit of decision making includes local—not district-office—control of the budget. As we saw in Chapter 3, in

1983 Purkey and Smith cited building-level autonomy as one important characteristic of an effective school. The unique mix of teacher strengths, student composition, community values, and the particular vision and goals of the principal and the staff requires local decision making. Lieberman (1988) noted that in some districts parents, teachers, administrators, and students together form planning groups to decide school-wide goals, needs for professional development, and "the general means for running the school."

A second component is *flexible scheduling* and use of time. Normally, flexible scheduling refers to manipulating hours and days more creatively to accommodate specific teaching needs and innovations. In one case, flexible scheduling included allowing a husband and wife to share one teaching position, with one teaching in the morning and the other taking over in the afternoon (Lieberman, 1988).

A third component is the development of a *collegial and participatory environment* among both students and staff (Lieberman, 1988). There is an increased personalization of the school environment that includes an atmosphere of trust, high expectations, and sense of fairness. We have seen these types of academic and social climate goals in every chapter of this book.

The fourth and fifth components complement and extend principles of effective schooling and teaching. The fourth component is a curriculum that helps students understand the *why* of what they are learning, not just the *what* and *how*. As the fifth component, teaching higher level *thinking skills* is finally becoming legitimized outside of special programs for gifted students. Such skills include creativity; critical thinking; analogical reasoning; categorizing; taking other points of view; Bloom's taxonomy skills of application, analysis, synthesis, and evaluation; and a host of others (e.g., Davis & Rimm, 1989).

It is refreshing to see the focus of effective schools broadened beyond improvements in mathematics and reading scores, although it will be some years before such outcomes as "understanding why," "creativity," and the like appear in newspapers school by school for public comparison and evaluation, as mathematics and reading scores currently do. One significant problem, as Stephans (1988) and Mack (1988) recently noted, is that good measures of many nonacademic school-effectiveness outcomes currently do not exist.

Finally, a component especially relevant to this chapter is the *changing role of the teacher* (e.g., McClure, 1988). Empowered teachers are seen as possessing more autonomy, more discretion, and more responsibility, particularly in working collaboratively with each other for improved teaching. For example, an excellent master teacher may teach children part time and work with other teachers part time.

Overall, then, the goals of second-wave reform stress building-level autonomy, more flexible use of time, fostering colleagueship, a more professional culture, higher expectations, teaching for understanding, teaching thinking skills, and expanded roles for teachers that include greater recognition and status and a reward structure that reinforces growing and learning. As Lieberman (1988) put it, "We have the potential to change the structure of the school itself and, in so doing, the nature of American education."

OBSERVATION AND COACHING AND TEACHER WORK GROUPS

Let us first consider the dynamics of administrator and peer observation and of teachers working together. That is, why exactly do these strategies seem to produce more enthusiastic, eager-to-learn, and professionally dedicated teachers? These teachers become better able to raise students' achievement levels, improve school attitudes, and reduce classroom behavior problems, all the while becoming better at self-examination, self-reflectiveness, and self-supervision (Cook, 1988).

In fact, there are many mechanisms through which observation and coaching by a principal or a colleague or participation in teacher work groups and teams can improve both teaching and the school climate.

Little (1987) outlined the following possible dynamics of teacher interaction to plan and improve teaching. First, lesson planning may improve when people press each other to explain exactly what they are doing and why they are doing it. By making teaching principles and practices more visible and more public, the best practices are promoted and the weakest ones discarded. Also, the toughest, most persistent problems of curriculum, instruction, and management get the benefit of the principal's or fellow teachers' experience. Moreover, there may be an increased sense of confidence and a felt obligation to do well. There is peer pressure to do a good teaching job, to live up to agreements made, and to implement ideas that have been offered.

The shared responsibility, increased interaction, and visibility of teaching plans and performances heighten the influence of teachers on one another and on the school. From the students' perspective, the visibility of teachers working together may deliver a motivating message; the students sense the increased concern, optimism, and expectations of the teachers. Finally, the close work with colleagues may promote stimulation and solidarity that reflect themselves in enthusiastic classroom performances and a reduction in frustration and burnout.

As Little (1987) admitted, the true explanation for the effectiveness of high collegiality, teamwork, and mutual assistance lies in some complex combination of all of these possibilities.

CLASSROOM OBSERVATION AND SUPERVISION BY PRINCIPALS

A central part of a principal's instructional leadership role is the direct observation and supervision of teachers in classrooms. The main purpose of classroom observation and the conference that follows is the improvement of teaching; a secondary purpose is to evaluate the teacher, for example, for tenure (Holland, 1988). A thorough explanation of the evaluative focus of observation by principals is beyond the focus of this book. Ubben and Hughes (1987), Sergiovanni (1987), and Blumberg and Greenfield (1986) are good resources for further reading on this subject.

As for the goals and outcomes of supervisor–teacher conferences, Holland (1988) emphasized that there are both direct and indirect influences on improving teaching. In the role of critic, expert, and connoisseur of good teaching (Cook, 1988), the supervisor will make direct suggestions for improving teaching or classroom management, perhaps commenting on starting a lesson more promptly, using more engaging objectives, picking up the pace, using more verbal reinforcement, facing the class, or using more interesting materials or demonstrations that the supervisor happens to know about.

The benefits may be indirect in the sense that such conferences help teachers become more reflective—more likely to examine their own teaching, think about why they do what they do, and think about what else they might do.

The following, then, pertains to observation by principals and assistant principals for the purpose of improving teachers' instructional and management skills.

Evaluation Cycle

As the concept of classroom observation by principals has evolved in recent years, it includes minor variations on the following steps, referred to as the *evaluation cycle:*

1. An *orientation meeting,* in which the evaluator and the teacher(s) review the procedures and purposes of the classroom observations and the forms that will be used. An intrinsic function of the orientation meeting is to foster the development of a positive and collegial supervisor—teacher relationship and to reduce any anxiety or resentment about the observation and its inherent hint of evaluation. The purpose is to improve teaching. Supervision should not be, as Blumberg (1987) once said, a "private cold war." There is, of course, a conflict between a bureaucratic, paternalistic approach and the more desirable collegial format.

2. A *preobservation conference,* in which the principal or assistant principal discusses details and goals of the observation with the individual teacher, as well as any materials needed in advance by the observer (e.g., lesson plans, workbooks, etc.).

3. *Announced classroom visits,* which are the scheduled classroom observations.

4. *Unannounced classroom visits,* which allow the administrator to observe teaching and management behaviors under more natural conditions, perhaps when new curricula or teaching strategies are being tried out.

5. A *postobservation conference,* in which the supervisor and the teacher analyze the findings and data from the observation.

6. A *summative evaluation*—the final statement (usually given in the spring) which includes agreed-upon job improvement targets resulting from the two or three (or more) observations made during the year.

THE BELOIT PLAN

As one model of how a school district structured and conducted its classroom observations in a reasonable and defensible fashion, the Beloit, Wisconsin, public school system is training its principals in the art of classroom instructional supervision. The carefully developed plan focuses on observing teachers and providing positive and constructive feedback to them. Note the *belief statement* in Inset 6-1 that focuses entirely on evaluation as a vehicle for instructional improvement.

Each experienced teacher is evaluated every 3 years; probationary teachers are evaluated twice during their first 3 years. The formal evaluation cycle includes two 30-minute observations during the fall term. The supervisor also conducts unscheduled classroom observations.

Orientation Meeting

As a first step, all teachers in a school attend an afternoon orientation meeting in which the principal explains in detail the purposes and procedures of the classroom observations, which will be conducted by the principal or an assistant principal. They will observe what the teacher does and says and what students do and say—all that occurs during a lesson. They will look for things to work on and improve. The goal is constructive instructional improvement, not firing teachers. The supervision will be conducted in a collegial, supportive, and cooperative manner.

During this orientation the principal explains the four-step formal evaluation cycle and the forms that will be used (Appendices 6-1, 6-2, and 6-3 at the end of this chapter). For each of the two classroom observations, the four steps include a planning conference, a preobservation conference, the formal observation, and a feedback conference.

Planning Conference

At the planning conference a mutually agreeable time is set for the 30-minute observation. The teacher is given the Preobservation Form (Appendix 6-1), which is to be filled out and returned to the

---

INSET 6-1

Philosophy of Evaluation
School District of Beloit, Wisconsin

WE BELIEVE that the purpose of evaluation is to promote educational excellence through improved performance.

WE BELIEVE that the role of the evaluator is to make measurable objective evaluations of strengths and weaknesses and to provide recommendations for improvement within a system that is valid, reliable and legally discriminating. The criteria and procedures used shall be consistent throughout the District.

WE BELIEVE staff development is essential to achieve the goals of improved performance. This staff development should be provided prior to implementation and continuously throughout the evaluation process.

WE BELIEVE that supervision and evaluation are ongoing processes. They should be conducted in a collegial, supportive and cooperative manner.

Prepared by the Teacher Performance Based Evaluation Committee, School District of Beloit; Dr. Sally Frudden, Educational Consultant, Iowa State University; and Dr. Frank L. McKinzie, Superintendent, School District of Beloit, Wisconsin. Reprinted by permission of the School District of Beloit, Wisconsin.

---

supervisor, along with a lesson plan and samples of any materials to be used, at least 1 day before the preobservation conference. The form asks the teacher to explain the instructional objectives and how they fit into the district guides, instructional strategies, learning activities, unusual group or individual circumstances, evaluation of the learning outcomes, and anything specific that the teacher may want monitored.

Preobservation Conference

At the preobservation conference, held at least 1 day before the scheduled observation, the contents of the Preobservation Form are discussed, any pertinent comments by the teacher or supervisor are entered onto the form, and the form is signed by both parties.

Formal Observation

During the formal observation, the supervisor makes notes of teacher and student behaviors, most of which will be relevant to the entries on the Teacher Formative/Summative Evaluation Report (Appendix 6-2). This report includes performances in the categories of teaching techniques, classroom management strategies, and professional responsibilities. Many entries derive directly from the literature on effective schools (Chapter 3), classroom management (Chapter 4), and effective teaching (Chapter 5), for example:

Provides successful learning experiences.

Uses a variety of methods and activities.

Uses reviews and previews.

Models the learning activities.

Provides guided practice.

Summarizes lessons.

Checks for understanding.

Provides feedback.

Monitors student progress.

Sets high (but appropriate) expectations.

Communicates clearly and logically.

Uses praise and encouragement.

Provides structuring comments to help clarify the lesson.

Moves efficiently from one activity to the next.

Maximizes time on task.

Manages disruptive behavior constructively.

Provides opportunities for students to receive recognition and improve their self-image.

Shows a willingness to meet with students and parents.

Feedback Conference

The feedback conference, held within 10 school days after the formal observation, allows the supervisor and the teacher to discuss the teacher's lesson. The conference includes praise for good teaching practices, which is both appropriate and important for morale, along with specific recommendations for improvement and continued growth. The Professional Growth Plan Form (Appendix 6-3), which may focus on teaching techniques, classroom management, or professional responsibilities, is used as a written record of the supervisor's reaction, containing recommendations for what will be done and how it will be done.

The principal or assistant principal prepares a written summary of the feedback conference, the content of which is discussed with the teacher at the time of the conference. The teacher receives a copy.

If the supervisor conducts an unscheduled observation, a written report is prepared and shared with the teacher within 5 school days of the observation.

The Teacher Formative/Summative Evaluation Report (Appendix 6-2) summarizes information from both scheduled and unscheduled observations along with information from such supporting data as lesson plans, grade books, student work, pre- and posttests, and any written complaints, concerns, or relevant comments. The report is discussed with the teacher before mid-February.

At the time of this writing, the Beloit plan is still in its beginning stages. Overall, however, the plan appears to be a cohesive and thoughtfully developed strategy for guiding the instructional leadership activities of the principal and constructively and positively improving the quality of teaching.

COMMENTS ON
THE FEEDBACK CONFERENCE

The supervisor—teacher conference has received considerable attention from educational administrators, due no doubt to its extreme importance and delicate nature. As Goldhammer (1971) put it, "All roads lead to the conference."

Holland (1988) presented an extensive review of the purposes and dynamics of the supervisory conference. The supervisor, Holland noted, must establish a good social—emotional climate that is collegial rather than bureaucratic, have skills in using data obtained during the observation, anticipate teachers' needs, and, most important, encourage teachers to analyze their own teaching behavior and plan their own improvement. The supervisor plans ahead to present findings on the teaching patterns and critical incidents for mutual analysis with the teacher. There is an implicit assumption that the supervisor and the teacher agree on an ideal model of teaching, which may not always be accurate. In the conference, the supervisor positively and constructively emphasizes the teacher's pedagogical strengths in addition to making suggestions for improvements and encouraging increased reflectiveness.

Cook (1988) noted that during the conference the supervisor and teacher talk, analyze, and explore. The teacher, especially, analyzes almost everything the supervisor mentions. There typically is very little, if any, negative behavior. Sometimes the conference ends before goals are set.

Cook described three interesting and amusing types of responses by teachers to supervisors' suggestions: disagreement with the suggestion, semi-agreement ("I'll do it next time the supervisor comes in!"), and full agreement. In the disagreement category, some likely teacher responses are as follows:

"Yes, but we can't do that."

"We thought of that already."

"No, thank you."

"You're wrong."

In the semi-agreement category are such evasive reactions as

"Yeah, okay."

"It sounds like a good idea."

In the full agreement category Cook described just a "Yes, I'll build that in" response. For full acceptance and implementation, teachers must believe in and be committed to the suggestions.

Principals and other supervisors develop subtle conference tactics to influence teachers to accept suggestions. For example, Grimmitt and Crehan (1988) described a "strategic tentativeness" in principals' efforts to suggest changes. That is, the principal would try to eliminate the sting of evaluation or criticism by cautiously phrasing salient points as though they were tentative (e.g., "You seemed to be unaware of students' behavior during the lesson; did you happen to notice what they were doing?"). Diplomatic principals also might rephrase statements into questions; speak as though they were "thinking out loud"; or try to sound like an earnest colleague (Grimmitt & Crehan, 1988). Some supervisors use humor when describing classroom incidents that require improvement or correction. For example, "The kid kept dropping his paint bottle . . . he clutched it to his little chest, but it just kept popping out!" (Message: Improve your instructions for transporting paint.) Some supervisors also will present suggestions as though they actually were ideas of other teachers, not their own observations and recommendations.

Is the conference truly a joint venture, or can it subtly smack of paternalism and manipulation? Probably both. The conference surely is intended to reach the supervisor's goal of improving teaching and increasing the teacher's reflectiveness, self-examination, and self-improvement; yet to be effective the outcome must be mutually agreed upon in a collegial and pleasant atmosphere. As Goldsberry (1988) said, manipulation does go on, but it is not necessarily bad.

INFORMAL SUPERVISOR OBSERVATION

As we have noted before, the importance of strong instructional leadership, including classroom visits to supportively and constructively improve teaching, has its roots in the classic studies of effective schools. Needless to say, those classroom observation procedures, which were conducted by highly effective principals, were hardly as formal and structured as, for example, those in the Beloit plan. It is conceivable that if good collegial relations are established between the administrative and teaching staff and among teachers and if the climate is such that everyone is conscious of school improvement, more informal observation and coaching procedures could be adopted, as in the original studies of effective schools (Chapter 3).

PEER SUPERVISION AND COACHING AND TEACHERS WORKING TOGETHER: AN OPTIMISTIC VIEW

Any assumption that today's teachers are somehow ineffective, inefficient time-clock punchers who value only their paychecks simply is not true. The vast majority of teachers are professionals who take pride in their work and strive for knowledge and skills that will enhance their instructional abilities. They want very much to continue learning to do their work more effectively, and they will work toward that end.

Every study of effective schooling and effective teaching has found many highly successful teachers. These are teachers who, through a combination of training, intuition, and trial and error, have come to use many of the principles and recommendations summarized in this book. They rework goals and philosophies necessary to keep their schools alive and current. They write and rewrite the curriculum and monitor it across age levels. They evaluate student progress and report the results to the principal. They work together on instructional problems, interconnecting for unity and harmony of purpose. They actively seek professional development.

Every description of good principals stresses their vision of what their schools can be—a vision that guides their instructional leadership activities. However, every motivated, successful teacher also creates a vision of what his or her students can accomplish and become. That vision is integrated with lesson goals and plans and specific strategies to raise achievement. It also is integrated with efforts to motivate students and teach good self-concepts, good citizenship, aesthetics, thinking skills, and other important nonbasics.

TEACHERS HELPING TEACHERS

The Beloit, Wisconsin, plan for supervision and improvement of instruction, which is representative of other evaluation-cycle approaches, is a highly formal and organized procedure. Following one or more orientation meetings, an individual preobservation conference is held, purposes and data recording forms are discussed, a lesson plan and materials are provided to the principal in advance, the classroom visit is held on schedule, relevant information is properly recorded, a postobservation conference is held, and eventually a formal evaluation report and perhaps a professional growth plan are prepared.

In contrast, the process of peer supervision and coaching is much more informal and relaxed. It does not require publicly stated steps and procedures and prepared forms. Because peer supervision is virtually always voluntary, there is never a need for union intervention to protect teachers' rights. (In contrast, grievances have been filed in response to principals' observation procedures, however well-intentioned and carefully planned they have been.)

The main categories of teachers working together, or *colleagueship* as Little (1987) called it, include, first, a classroom observation and coaching process resembling the principals' visits described in the previous section. The observing teacher might even videotape his or her colleague in action, collecting data for later analysis and comment.* Second, many dynamic schools form teacher work groups that meet weekly to discuss and solve problems and plan and install new teaching methods. If the school uses team teaching, the group may meet daily for "reflection in action" (Sykes, 1983). Third, *teacher centers* are a less often used plan that, as the name suggests, involves group meetings with an expert teacher, consultant, other professional, or just peers to improve teaching methods and management skills.

Whatever its form, there is good evidence that strong colleagueship—working together—can lead to improved teaching, better professional relations among teachers, high job satisfaction, and improved student achievement and school attitudes.

Teacher Centers

Some school districts have supported peer supervision and coaching through the creation of teacher centers (Lieberman, 1988). Originally a British idea (Thornbury, 1974), teacher centers

---

*Imagine for a moment the impact of a principal's announcing to union-conscious teachers that their classroom performances will be videotaped. At the least, camera-shy teachers would become anxious. At worst, the threat of videotaped evidence for censure or dismissal would raise the hackles of the entire teaching staff, particularly the union representative.

are "places where teachers can come together with other teachers, and perhaps with other useful persons, such as professors, to do things that will help them teach better" (Gage, 1978). Although first conceived in the 1970s, teacher centers are becoming a viable approach to improving teaching effectiveness in the 1990s.

To create and operate a teacher center, administrators and teachers must work together. For example, support by the district administrator and building administrator are needed to arrange release time for both teacher-instructors and teacher-students. Gage (1978), however, argued that teacher centers are best initiated and controlled by teachers themselves, rather than being a type of forced and mandated inservice training. Administrators, professors, and parents, Gage said, "should come only by invitation. . . . Teachers should have the right to do the job for themselves." Teacher centers will survive only if they succeed in both improving teaching and favorably impressing participants, Gage noted.

Teacher centers are likely to focus on teaching strategies and materials in specific subject areas for specific student groups and on classroom management. Several formats have been tried. With the *encounter approach,* a secure and supportive setting is created where teachers informally share their problems, solutions, and teaching expertise with one another. Alternatively, the center may use expert teachers and workshop leaders who present new ideas, materials, and strategies. This more *directive approach* intrinsically encourages teachers to reexamine their beliefs about teaching and the ways they organize their classrooms and instructional methods. According to Gage (1978), "teacher centers can [include] . . . discussion and encounter groups, workshops, advisory services, and the simple process of helping teachers talk to one another."

Peer Supervision versus Administrator Supervision

To some, the top-down nature of many school improvement programs, combined with the often-repeated emphasis on the instructional leadership of the principal, seems to tacitly assume that teachers are not capable of improving their own teaching effectiveness. Therefore, the responsibility for assessing teaching, recommending changes, and enforcing those recommendations has fallen to the principal. This approach appears to be paternalistic. It does not seem to encourage autonomous, competent teachers to be responsible for their own professional improvement or for the development of their colleagues (Dillon-Peterson, 1986).

In fact, dedicated and professionally motivated teachers can and do work together to improve each other's teaching and management skills, and they give each other more than just social support. They become partners in planning goals and strategies for school-wide improvement programs. They consult each other on teaching and management problems, often taking a problem-solving approach of clarifying the problem and then brainstorming solutions. They observe and critique each other in classrooms.

When the initiative for improvement comes from the teachers themselves, chances are good that the attitudinal climate of the entire school will improve and that the teachers will, in fact, take increasing responsibility for their own growth (Bang-Jensen, 1986).

Bang-Jensen put forth a good argument for peer supervision, claiming that it is more effective, more efficient, and more rewarding than hierarchical supervision by an administrator. Because of other strong demands on the principal's time, Bang-Jensen noted, classroom observation, if it occurs at all, usually is limited to once or twice per year, which does not help teachers learn and grow on a continual basis. Furthermore, observation and supervision carried out for the purpose of improving teaching are clouded by the inseparable element of evaluation.

In fact, some teachers play it safe by repeating their successful prerehearsed and staged performances for the supervisor. Unions and school boards, ever mindful of teachers' rights, have demanded that teachers receive plenty of notice before each formal observation/evaluation. However, when a teacher is observed informally by a fellow teacher for the sole purpose of growth, there is freedom to take risks—to design lessons that might produce unexpected outcomes or even failure. A common trait of successful innovators is a willingness to fail and, in fact, a high rate of actual failure (Davis, 1986). According to peer supervisor Bang-Jensen, one teacher reported that she "learned the most from our attempts that didn't work."

The Peer Supervisor

Nonthreatening empathy and high credibility are two important traits of the peer supervisor. A fellow teacher is selected to observe and help because of his or her expertise in teaching a subject area. The authority is based solely on the colleague's perception that the peer can help him or her develop more effective strategies and resources. As one teacher said, "I asked you to work with me because, in observing you last year, [I saw that] you had something specific that I wanted" (Bang-Jensen, 1986). Further, the peer supervisor understands the impact of district and school policies and even knows the needs of specific children.

The availability of the expert peer in the building also is a plus. However, that availability does demand release time, and therefore it requires the support of the superintendent and the principal, particularly in funding a teacher assistant to substitute for about 45 minutes per supervising day.

Peer Supervision Process

One of the first steps in peer supervision is assessing the other teachers' needs in order to determine what is to be worked on. These needs may be identified by asking the teacher about his or her specific problems and goals for improvement and by discussing the quality and level of student work. Teachers' needs also can be evaluated by classroom observation. The observer would watch for violations of principles of effective teaching and management that are interfering with teaching and learning or for instances when different materials, techniques, or activities would aid learning.

Peer supervision always is congenial and informal. Teachers discuss how they will work together, when and how they will observe each other, and the manner of providing feedback. They also might set a few immediate short-term objectives such as ways to stimulate student interest and involvement with particular lessons.

During the actual observation, the peer supervisor notes such things as whether the room arrangement is ideal for each learning activity; when students are sharing their ideas or stories with each other; signs of boredom and inattention, often related to the duration and interest value of specific activities; and the appropriateness and variety of materials and activities. The peer supervisor also observes the teacher's methods of explaining purposes and objectives, reviewing, organizing, presenting information, questioning, encouraging turn taking, directing work, providing feedback and reinforcement, and so forth.

One effective way to provide feedback to the observed teacher is to use open-ended questions such as the following:

What were you trying to do? What was the objective of the lesson?

How did you determine that this was the appropriate level of difficulty for these students?

How did you select the materials to be used in today's lesson?

What is your evaluation of the lesson?

What did you think went well?

What would you like to improve?

These kinds of self-examination questions, combined with information derived from the observation, lead to suggestions that help the observed teacher understand areas of strength and weakness.

Long-term growth will be aided if the peer supervision includes follow-up practice and coaching and if additional peer supervision is provided to foster further development of new skills and behaviors (Rodriguez & Johnstone, 1986).

BENEFITS OF TEACHER OBSERVATION AND COACHING AND WORK GROUPS

A teacher observation and coaching program must be perceived as beneficial by the principal who helps organize and promote the plan, the superintendent who must agree to it, the school board that pays for it, the expert teachers who must put aside other matters in order to work with their colleagues, and the teacher-participants themselves. All must be convinced that the benefits are cost-effective when compared to other teaching-improvement alternatives (Little, 1987). The consensus seems to be that such programs work very well indeed.

The most visible benefit of teacher observation and coaching is a continued and steady improvement of teaching over time. As Little (1987) put it, in schools with high levels of professional collaboration, "ordinary people, relying on ordinary budgets and confronted with the ordinary ebb and flow of energy, goodwill, and creativity, accomplish extraordinary things. . . . Something is gained when teachers work together, and something is lost when they do not."

Furthermore, when teachers work together for improvement, strong collegiality and solid professional relationships develop. Little (1987) noted that "recognition and satisfaction stem not only from becoming a masterful teacher but also from being a member of a masterful group."

Bird and Little (1985) described a junior high school teacher work group whose revisions in curriculum, testing, and student placement procedures led to remarkable gains in mathematics achievement and the virtual elimination of classroom behavior problems. Little (1981) described an elementary school whose school-wide academic gains were attributed to weekly teacher meetings in which teachers learned and installed mastery procedures. According to Little (1987), the teachers in these studies agreed that the benefits of working together far outweighed the advantages of working alone. The quality and coherence of the programs improved, as did faculty cohesiveness. Moreover, students perceived the faculty cohesiveness and the consistency in achievement expectations.

Cohen (1981) reported that teacher collaboration improved their capacity to understand and apply new curriculum ideas, methods, and materials. Generally, greater complexity (variability) in curricula has been a recurrent benefit of teacher group work. Teachers learn to refine and improve existing curricula and select and implement new curricula on a continuing basis.

Curriculum is not the only focus of change, of course. Groups plan improvements in classroom management techniques, testing procedures, and student placement policies. Little (1987) concluded that teacher collaboration and mutual help lead to "an expanded pool of ideas, materials, and methods and a collective ability to generate higher-quality solutions to problems." Some common outcomes of peer teaching and colleagueship include the following (Bang-Jensen, 1986; Little, 1981, 1987; Little & Bird, 1984):

- Higher rates of innovation, coherence, and vitality in the curriculum.

- Greater frequency and depth of discussion about instructional and management issues, that is, greater collegiality.

- Higher levels of enthusiasm for teaching.

- A reasonable mentoring approach to helping new teachers become proficient.

- Demonstrated student gains in achievement and in affective and social areas.

Other positive effects of administrator and/or peer supervision and work groups were discussed earlier in this chapter, for example, increased visibility and pressure to do well, shared responsibility, the "natural selection" of the best teaching principles, and a positive impact on students of seeing dedicated teachers work together to improve instruction. We also noted that peer supervision, compared to supervision by an administrator, can be more effective, more efficient, and more rewarding.

POTENTIAL PROBLEMS

Teacher work groups and peer teaching can fail, however. For example, if the initial clumsy and awkward efforts are unsuccessful, such meetings and procedures will be abandoned in favor of more familiar routines (Bredo, 1975, 1977). Little (1987) noted that some critics have argued that pressure for group work leads only to unproductive compliance to mediocre ideas and that the extensive out-of-class time required is not justifiable.

Research at Stanford University (Little & Bird, 1984) confirmed that the mere existence of teacher work groups does not guarantee that the teacher-participants will reach a level of instructional sophistication that they could not reach by working alone. At the same time, however, this research confirmed that a proficient and well-organized teacher group that perceives its purpose and obligations and works to shape its tasks and outcomes will indeed produce results greater than the accomplishments of the individual teacher.

THE PROCESS OF CHANGE

While everyone wants immediate results, and some visible changes can indeed be made immediately, the process of improving overall school effectiveness is a slow one. The usual projection is that a period of 3 to 5 years is needed to change a school climate and develop and implement major new programs. The attitudes of administrators, staff, and students must be molded into a culture that focuses on, values, and rewards high academic achievement. Teachers and other staff must become conscious of and sensitive to the concept of school improvement. They must help plan and implement specific school-improvement ideas such as new curricula, classroom observation by supervisors or peers, selection of in-service workshops, or other options.

An old joke asks "How many psychiatrists does it take to change a light bulb?" The answer is: "Just one, but the light bulb has to want to change." The same applies to increasing the effectiveness of the individual teacher. Apart from any district-wide or school-wide formal improvement program, an individual teacher who wishes to improve his or her skills must be highly motivated (and sufficiently secure) to engage in self-examination and self-improvement.

There will be resistance. McClure (1988) pointed out that there seems to be an 11th Commandment: "You will keep school the way it has always been!" There is much conservatism among teachers, due partly to reactions against the types of innovations foisted on them in the 1960s (McClure, 1988). Reform critic Cuban (1988) noted that "teachers adapt to cope with difficult work place conditions, and that is why they teach the way they do." He further argued that only a minority will change their teaching. Said Cuban, "There always are a couple of teachers with a self-renewing mechanism who will want to change what they are doing."

But let us be optimistic and, we feel, realistic. Effective schools have been created, and they *can* be created. In the words of Ronald Edmonds (1979), "We already know more than we need . . . to successfully teach all children whose schooling is of interest to us."

SUMMARY

Strong instructional leadership by the principal is one of the most recurrent characteristics of effective schools. Empowered teachers can and will take responsibility for their own professional development.

Traditionally, teachers have worked in isolation, with beginning teachers receiving little assistance. "One-way teaching" amounts to planning, presenting, and keeping order. It is inconsistent with a better conception of teaching that emphasizes understanding students, the subject matter, learning, and schooling; exemplifying attitudes of inquiry and critical thinking; teaching for understanding and for mastery; and coping successfully with complex classroom social relations.

Teacher shortages make instructional leadership—saving the "bad apples"—especially important. Poor teaching may be due to inadequate supervision rather than lack of ability or effort. Principals are managers of experts; all must work in harmony and unity in an atmosphere that values achievement.

Deal and Kennedy described characteristics of corporate leadership and cultures that have clear implications for education. A strong, coherent, and meaningful culture sets guiding values and improves morale and productivity. Successful corporations identify heroes to emulate, install rituals and ceremonies, and recognize the informal communication network.

Second-wave reform builds upon effective schooling concepts in emphasizing school site management; more flexible use of time; a collegial and participatory environment; higher expectations; teaching for understanding (the "why"); teaching thinking skills; and an expanded and more autonomous (empowered) role for teachers, who work together to improve teaching.

The dynamics of observation and coaching and teacher work groups include a combination of improved lesson planning; group solutions to the most difficult problems; increased confidence and a felt obligation to do well; pressure to live up to agreements and implement ideas; elimination of weak teaching strategies; increased enthusiasm and reduced burnout; and a perception of increased teacher concern that motivates students.

The main purpose of classroom observation is to improve teaching; a secondary purpose is teacher evaluation. It can provide both direct effects on teaching improvement, in the form of specific supervisor suggestions for improvement, and indirect effects in the form of increased reflectiveness and self-improvement.

Classroom observation and coaching by supervisors includes the following evaluation cycle: an orientation meeting, a preobservation conference (perhaps preceded by a planning conference), announced classroom visits, unannounced classroom visits, a postobservation (feedback) conference, and an end-of-the-year summative evaluation.

As illustrated in the Beloit, Wisconsin, plan, much of the observation focuses on principles of effective schooling, effective teaching, and classroom management, along with professional responsibilities. The feedback conference is important yet delicate.

The supervisor must establish a good collegial atmosphere, present his or her findings, emphasize the teacher's strengths, and encourage the teacher to use improved teaching methods. Together, the supervisor and teacher analyze and explore.

Teachers can respond by disagreeing with suggestions, partially agreeing, or fully agreeing. Supervisors can use subtle, or diplomatic, tactics to influence teachers to accept suggestions, for example, using so-called strategic tentativeness, rephrasing statements into questions, using humor, or presenting suggestions as though they came from other teachers. The manipulation is not necessarily bad.

The majority of today's teachers are informed and motivated professionals who take pride in their work and strive for continued professional development.

Three ways that teachers can work together include the following:

1. Classroom observation and coaching, which is much more informal than observation by a supervisor.

2. Teacher work groups or teams that meet weekly or daily to solve problems or plan and implement new curricula and teaching methods.

3. Teacher centers can include encounter groups of teachers who share problem solutions and teaching expertise or workshops led by expert teachers or other professionals.

Peer observation and coaching can be more effective, more efficient, and more rewarding than hierarchical supervision by an administrator. Peers have more time for supervising fellow teachers. Some teachers present well-rehearsed, staged performances when observed by a supervisor. They feel more free to experiment when supervised by a peer.

Peer supervisors should possess empathy and have high credibility—a perceived ability to share valued expertise. They assess other teachers' needs through discussion and observation of such matters as room arrangement; signs of boredom; suitability of materials and activities; and methods of reviewing, presenting objectives, presenting information, and so on.

Teacher observation and teacher work group strategies must be perceived by administrators and teachers as beneficial and cost-effective.

Evidence reported by Little and others indicates that when teachers work together strong colleagueship and professional relations develop, along with higher enthusiasm for teaching. Teaching continues to improve, student achievement and school attitudes improve, innovation rates are higher, curriculum complexity (variety) improves, and other teaching components are improved and modified, for example, classroom management skills and testing and placement procedures.

Teacher work groups can fail, particularly if the initial efforts are unsuccessful. However, if teacher work groups perceive their purpose and work to shape outcomes, the results will be better than accomplishments of individuals.

While some improvements can be made immediately, improving the school climate and implementing new programs may require 3 to 5 years or longer. There will be resistance to change. However, an individual motivated teacher can improve his or her professional skills more quickly, perhaps guided by the kinds of teaching and management principles presented in this book.

APPENDICES TO CHAPTER 6

Appendices 6-1, 6-2, and 6-3 were prepared by the Teacher Performance Based Evaluation Committee, School District of Beloit; Dr. Sally Frudden, Educational Consultant, Iowa State University; and Dr. Frank L. McKenzie, Superintendent, School District of Beloit, Wisconsin. Reprinted by permission of the School District of Beloit, Wisconsin.

APPENDIX 6-1

Teacher Preobservation Form

The preobservation form shall be given to the teacher at least three (3) school days prior to the Preobservation Conference. The completed preobservation form shall be submitted to the supervisor at least one (1) day prior to the Preobservation Conference.

Teacher's Name	Class Observed	Grade Level	Date	Time

PREOBSERVATION DATA

EVALUATOR'S – COMMENTS

I. What are the instructional objectives for this lesson?

II. How does this lesson fit into the district's course of study? (Introductory, middle, or culminating activity) Explain.

III. What instructional strategy(ies) do you plan to use for this lesson (examples; lecture, small group discussion, question/answer, etc.) and why?

IV. What learning activities will the students be doing?

V. Are there any group or individual characteristics or circumstances of which the evaluator should be aware? (unusual behaviors, group interactions, etc.) _____ yes _____ no   Explain.

VI. How will you determine if the learner outcomes have been reached?

VII. Are there specific performance areas/criteria you want monitored?

Attach a copy of lesson plans and samples of materials to be used during the teaching activity.

Evaluatee's Comments:

Evaluator's Comments:

_____   _____
Evaluatee's Signature   Date

_____   _____
Evaluator's Signature   Date

APPENDIX 6-2

Teacher Formative/Summative Evaluation Report

TEACHER'S NAME _____   BUILDING ASSIGNMENT _____

DIRECTIONS:

1. Beside each criterion, please check the phrase which best describes the evaluatee's performance on that item.

2. Written comments must follow each criterion rating.

PERFORMANCE AREA 1: PRODUCTIVE TEACHING TECHNIQUES

A.

☐ DOES NOT MEET DISTRICT STANDARDS   ☐ IS INCONSISTENT IN MEETING DISTRICT STANDARDS   ☐ MEETS DISTRICT STANDARDS

COMMENTS:

A. Demonstrates Effective Planning Skills

1. Selects appropriate long/short-range goals.

2. Uses instructional objectives that are related to long/short-range goals and prescribed curriculum.

3. Selects objectives at the correct level of difficulty to provide successful learning experiences.

4. Selects a variety of teaching methods and procedures along with a variety of student activities relevant to the objective.

5. Selects or creates materials to use as appropriate.

APPENDIX 6-2 (Continued)

B.

☐ DOES NOT MEET DISTRICT STANDARDS ☐ IS INCONSISTENT IN MEETING DISTRICT STANDARDS ☐ MEETS DISTRICT STANDARDS

COMMENTS:

B. Implements The Lesson Plan

1. Uses a preparatory set which may include review and preview.

2. States instructional objectives.

3. Provides input related to objectives.

4. Models activities congruent with topic being taught and provides guided practice to reinforce concepts.

5. Utilizes lesson summary techniques.

6. Checks for understanding

C.

☐ DOES NOT MEET DISTRICT STANDARDS ☐ IS INCONSISTENT IN MEETING DISTRICT STANDARDS ☐ MEETS DISTRICT STANDARDS

COMMENTS:

C. Provides students with specific evaluative feedback, monitors and adjusts as individual differences warrant.

1. Gives written comments, as well as points or scores as appropriate.

2. Returns test results as quickly as possible.

3. Makes opportunities for one to one conferences.

4. Administers criterion-referenced pre- and posttests, and standardized tests as appropriate.

5. Interprets tests results to students and parents.

6. Makes methods of evaluation clear and purposeful.

7. Monitors student progress through a series of formative and summative evaluation techniques.

☐ DOES NOT MEET DISTRICT STANDARDS	☐ IS INCONSISTENT IN MEETING DISTRICT STANDARDS	☐ MEETS DISTRICT STANDARDS

COMMENTS:

D.

D. Sets high expectations for student achievement.

1. Establishes expectations for students based on a level of skills acquisition appropriate to their ability level.

2. Promotes personal goal setting.

☐ DOES NOT MEET DISTRICT STANDARDS	☐ IS INCONSISTENT IN MEETING DISTRICT STANDARDS	☐ MEETS DISTRICT STANDARDS

COMMENTS:

E.

E. Communicates effectively with students.

1. Speaks clearly.

2. Communicates ideas and directions clearly and logically.

3. Uses a variety of verbal and nonverbal techniques.

4. Praises, elicits and responds to student questions before proceeding.

5. Utilizes probing techniques.

6. Provides structuring comments which clarify the tasks and help the lesson proceed smoothly.

APPENDIX 6-2 (Continued)

PERFORMANCE AREA II: ORGANIZED, STRUCTURED CLASS MANAGEMENT

	DOES NOT MEET DISTRICT STANDARDS	IS INCONSISTENT IN MEETING DISTRICT STANDARDS	MEETS DISTRICT STANDARDS

A.

COMMENTS:

A. Plans for and makes effective use of time, materials and resources.

1. Indicates positive directions for moving from one activity to the next.

2. Uses materials effectively and efficiently.

3. Maximizes time on task.

	DOES NOT MEET DISTRICT STANDARDS	IS INCONSISTENT IN MEETING DISTRICT STANDARDS	MEETS DISTRICT STANDARDS

B.

COMMENTS:

B. Sets high standards for student behavior and responsibility.

1. Manages discipline problems in accordance with administrative regulations, school board policies and legal requirements.

2. Establishes and clearly communicates parameters for student classroom behavior and promotes self-discipline.

3. Manages disruptive behavior constructively.

4. Demonstrates fairness and consistency in the handling of student problems.

5. Helps students develop efficient learning skills and work habits.

6. Creates a climate in which students display initiative and assume a personal responsibility for learning.

192

PERFORMANCE AREA III: PROFESSIONAL RESPONSIBILITIES

A.

	DOES NOT MEET DISTRICT STANDARDS	IS INCONSISTENT IN MEETING DISTRICT STANDARDS	MEETS DISTRICT STANDARDS

COMMENTS:

A. Establishes and maintains a working relationship with parents, students and school personnel.

1. Provides a climate which establishes rapport and opens up communications.

2. Deals with exceptional educational and health needs of students.

3. Provides opportunities for all students to achieve positive recognition and improve self-image.

4. Displays a willingness to meet with students, school personnel and parents as appropriate.

5. Communicates effectively with administrators and/or appropriate school personnel concerning school related matters.

APPENDIX 6-2 (Continued)

| ☐ DOES NOT MEET DISTRICT STANDARDS | ☐ IS INCONSISTENT IN MEETING DISTRICT STANDARDS | ☐ MEETS DISTRICT STANDARDS |

B.

COMMENTS:

B. Demonstrates employee responsibilities

1. Supports and participates in parent-teacher activities.

2. Uses discretion in handling confidential information.

3. Reports suspected cases of substance abuse and child abuse.

4. Is punctual.

5. Exercises reasonable responsibility for student management through the building.

6. Follows school policies and regulations.

7. Completes duties promptly and accurately.

8. Provides an appropriate role model.

9. Respects the rights and views of others.

10. Keeps abreast of the latest theories and knowledge in the area of assignment throughout attendance at conferences, workshops, staff meetings, college or university courses or personal reading, in accordance with Board policy.

☐ Probation ☐ Non Probationary

Evaluatee's Signature* _____ Date _____

☐ Re-employment is recommended ☐ Re-employment is not recommended

Evaluator's Signature _____ Date _____

* Although I do not necessarily agree with all the ratings and statement included herein, I have had the opportunity to review the contents of this instrument and have been given the opportunity to clarify my position to those areas where agreement was not achieved.

194

APPENDIX 6–3

Professional Growth Plan

THE TEACHER SHALL NOT BE SUBJECT TO MORE THAN THREE (3) PROFESSIONAL GROWTH TARGETS AT ONE TIME PER EVALUATION CYCLE.

NAME	SUBJECT/GRADE	BUILDING	DATE

PERFORMANCE AREA: (check one)

__ Productive Teaching Technique

__ Organized, Structured Classroom Management

__ Professional Responsibilities

Criterion from Summative Evaluation Report on which TARGET is based:

I. GOAL (general intent)

================================ PROFESSIONAL GROWTH TARGET ================================

II. SPECIFIC MEASURABLE BEHAVIOR   (What will be done?)

III. PROCEDURES: (How will it be done?)
Steps:

When to be accomplished

IV. PROGRESS CHECKS: (How is it going?)

EVALUATEE'S COMMENTS: EVALUATOR'S COMMENTS:

Signature _____ Date _____   Signature _____ Date _____

V. DOCUMENTATION/APPRAISAL METHOD FOR FINAL ACCOMPLISHMENT OF TARGET: (How do you know it was done?)

Written evidence

Appraisal method

Standard(s)

EVALUATEE'S COMMENTS:

EVALUATOR'S COMMENTS:

The target was:

___ Not accomplished
___ Partially accomplished
___ Fully accomplished

Evaluatee's Signature   Date

Evaluator's Signature   Date

References

Achilles, C. M. (1987). A vision of better schools. In W. D. Greenfield (Ed.), *Instructional leadership: Concepts, issues and controversies*. Boston: Allyn & Bacon.

Airasian, P. W., Kellaghan, T., & Madaus, G. F. (1979). *Concepts of school effectiveness as derived from research strategies: Differences in the findings*. Boston: Boston College.

Alloway, N. (1984). *Teacher expectations*. Paper presented at the Australian Association for Research in Education Annual Conference, Perth, Australia.

Anderson, B. O. (1978). The effects of long wait-time on high school physics pupils' response length, classroom attitudes and achievement. *Dissertation Abstracts International, 39*, 3493A. (University Microfilms No. 78–23, 871)

Anderson, L., Evertson, C. M., & Brophy, J. E. (1979). An experimental study of effective teaching in first-grade reading groups. *Elementary School Journal, 79*, 193–223.

Anderson, L., Evertson, C. M., & Brophy, J. E. (1982). *Principles of small-group instruction in elementary reading* (Occasional paper No. 58). East Lansing: Michigan State University, Institute for Research on Teaching.

Anderson, L., Evertson, C. M., & Emmer, E. (1980). Dimensions in classroom management derived from recent research. *Journal of Curriculum Studies, 12*, 343–356.

Arlin, M. (1979). Teacher transitions can disrupt time flow in classrooms. *American Educational Research Journal, 16*, 42–56.

Armor, D., Conry-Oseguera, P., Cox, M., King, N., McDonnell, L., Pascal, A., Pauly, E., & Zellman, G. (1976). *Analysis of the school preferred reading program in selected Los Angeles minority schools*. Santa Monica, CA: Rand Corporation.

Austin, G. R. (1979). Exemplary schools and the search for effectiveness. *Educational Leadership, 37*(1), 10–14.

Austin, G. R., & Garber, H. (Eds.). (1985). *Research on exemplary schools*. New York: Academic Press.

Austin, G. R., & Holowenzak, S. P. (1985). An examination of 10 years of research on exemplary schools. In G. R. Austin & H. Garber (Eds.), *Research on exemplary schools.* New York: Academic Press.

Ausubel, D. A. (1978). In defense of advance organizers: A reply to the critics. *Review of Educational Research, 48*, 162–178.

Averch, H. A., Carroll, S. J., Donaldson, T. S., Kiesling, H. J., & Pincus, J. (1974). *How effective is schooling? A critical review*. Englewood Cliffs, NJ: Educational Technology Publications.

Bang-Jensen, V. (1986). The view from next door: A look at peer "supervision." In K. K. Zumwalt (Ed.), *Improving teaching: 1986 ASCD yearbook*. Alexandria, VA: Association for Supervision and Curriculum Development.

Barr, R. C. (1980, March). *School, class, group, and pace effects on learning*. Paper presented at the annual meeting of the American Educational Research Association, Boston, MA.

Berliner, D. C. (1984). The half-full glass: A review of research on teaching. In P. L. Hosford (Ed.), *Using what we know about teaching*. Reston, VA: Virginia Association for Supervision and Curriculum Development.

Berliner, D. C. (1985). Effective classroom teaching: The necessary but not sufficient condition for developing exemplary schools. In G. R. Austin & H. Garber (Eds.), *Research on exemplary schools*. New York: Academic Press.

Berliner, D. C. (1986a). In pursuit of the expert pedagogue. *Educational Researcher, 15*(7), 5–13.

Berliner, D. C. (1986b, November/December). When kids "do seatwork," what do they do? *Instructor,* 14–15.

Berliner, D. C. (1987). But do they understand? In V. Richardson-Koehler (Ed.), *Educators' handbook: A research perspective*. New York: Longman.

Berliner, D. C., Fisher, C., Filby, N., & Marliave, R. (1978). *Executive summary of Beginning Teacher Evaluation Study*. San Francisco: Far West Laboratory for Educational Research and Development.

Berliner, D. C., & Tikunoff, W. (1976). The California Beginning Teacher Evaluation Study: Overview of the ethnographic study. *Journal of Teacher Education, 27*(1), 24–30.

Berliner, D. C., & Tikunoff, W. (1977). Ethnography in the classroom. In G. Borich & K. Fenton (Eds.), *The appraisal of teaching: Concepts and process*. Reading, MA: Addison-Wesley.

Bickel, W. E. (1983). Effective schools: Knowledge, dissemination, inquiry. *Educational Researcher, 12*(4), 3–5.

Bird, T. D., & Little, J. W. (1985). *Instructional leadership in eight secondary schools*. (Final report to the National Institute of Education). Boulder, CO: Center for Action Research.

Bloom, B. S. (Ed.). (1974). *Taxonomy of educational objectives*. New York: McKay.

Blum, R. E. (1984). *Effective schooling practices: A research synthesis*. Portland, OR: Northwest Regional Educational Laboratory.

Blumberg, A. (1987). The work of principals: A touch of craft. In W. D. Greenfield (Ed.), *Instructional leadership: Concepts, issues, and controversies*. Boston: Allyn & Bacon.

Blumberg, A., & Greenfield, W. D. (1980). *The effective principal*. Newton, MA: Allyn & Bacon.

Blumberg, A., & Greenfield, W. D. (1986). *The effective principal* (2nd ed.). Newton, MA: Allyn & Bacon.

Boeck, M. A., & Hillenmeyer, G. P. (1973, March). *Classroom interaction patterns during microteaching: Wait time as an instructional variable*. Paper presented at the annual meeting of the American Educational Research Association, New Orleans.

Bondi, J., & Wiles, J. (1986). School reform in Florida—Implications for the middle school. *Educational Leadership, 44*(1), 44–49.

Bowles, S. S., & McGintis, J. (1976). *Schooling in capitalist America: Educational reform and the contradictions of economic life.* New York: Basic Books.

Brady, M. E., Clinton, D., Sweeney, J. M., Peterson, M., & Poyner, H. (1977). *Instructional dimensions study.* Washington, DC: Kirschner Associates.

Bredo, E. (1975). *Collaborative relationships on teaching problems: Implications for collegial influence, team morale, and instructional practices.* (Technical Report No. 45). Stanford, CA: Stanford University Center for Research and Development in Teaching.

Bredo, E. (1977). Collaborative relations among elementary school teachers. *Sociology of Education, 50,* 300–309.

Bridges, E. M. (1986). *The incompetent teacher: The challenge and the response.* New York: Taylor & Francis.

Brookover, W. B. (1981). Why do some urban schools succeed? The Phi Delta Kappa study of exceptional urban elementary schools. *Harvard Educational Review, 51,* 439–441.

Brookover, W. B., Beady, C., Flood, P., Schweitzer, J., & Wisenbaker, J. (1979). *School social systems and student achievement: Schools can make a difference.* New York: Praeger.

Brookover, W. B., Beamer, L., Efthim, H., Hathaway, D., Lezotte, L., Miller, S., Passalacqua, J., & Tornatzky, L. (1982). *Creating effective schools: An inservice program for enhancing school learning climate and achievement.* Holmes Beach, FL: Learning Publications.

Brookover, W. B., & Lezotte, L. (1979). *Changes in school characteristics coincident with changes in student achievement.* East Lansing: Michigan State University, Institute for Research on Teaching. (ERIC Document Reproduction Service No. ED 181 005).

Brooks, D. M. (1985). Beginning the year in junior high: The first day of school. *Educational Leadership, 42*(8), 76–78.

Brooks, D. M., & Hawke, G. (1985, March). *Effective and ineffective session-opening teacher activity and task structures.* Paper presented at the annual meeting of the American Educational Research Association, Chicago.

Brophy, J. E. (1979). Teacher behavior and its effects. *Journal of Educational Psychology, 71,* 733–750.

Brophy, J. E. (1982). How teachers influence what is taught and learned in classrooms. *Elementary School Journal, 83,* 1–13.

Brophy, J. E. (1983). Classroom organization and management. *Elementary School Journal, 83,* 265–286.

Brophy, J. E., & Evertson, C. M. (1974a). *Process-product correlations in the Texas Teacher Effectiveness Study: Final Report* (Research Report No. 74-4). Austin: Research and Development Center for Teacher Education, University of Texas.

Brophy, J. E., & Evertson, C. M. (1974b). *The Texas Teacher Effectiveness Project: Presentation of non-linear relationships and summary discussion* (Research Report No. 74-6). Austin: Research and Development Center for Teacher Education, University of Texas.

Brophy, J. E., & Evertson, C. M. (1976). *Learning from teaching: A developmental perspective.* Boston: Allyn & Bacon.

Brophy, J. E., & Good, T. L. (1970). Teachers' communication of differential expectations for children's classroom performance: Some behavioral data. *Journal of Educational Psychology, 61,* 365–375.

Brophy, J. E., & Good, T. L. (1974). *Teacher-student relationships.* New York: Holt.

Brophy, J. E., & Good, T. L. (1985). Teacher behavior and student achievement. In M. E. Wittrock (Ed.), *Handbook of research on teaching* (3rd ed.). Chicago: Rand-McNally.

Burlingame, M. (1987). Images of leadership in effective schools literature. In W. D. Greenfield (Ed.), *Instructional leadership: Concepts, issues, and controversies.* Boston: Allyn & Bacon.

Burns, R. B. (1984). How time is used in elementary schools: The activity structure of classrooms. In L. W. Anderson (Ed.), *Time and school learning: Theory, research and practice.* London: Croom Helm.

Buttram, J. S., & Kruse, J. (1988, April). *Critical ingredients for school improvement efforts.* Paper presented at the annual meeting of the American Educational Research Association, New Orleans.

Calderhead, J. (1983, March). *Research into teachers' and student teachers' cognitions: Exploring the nature of classroom practice.* Paper presented at the annual meeting of the American Educational Research Association, Montreal.

Charles, C. M. (1983). *Elementary classroom management.* New York: Longman.

Clark, T. A., & McCarthy, D. P. (1983). School improvement in New York City: The evolution of a project. *Educational Researcher, 12*(4), 17–24.

Cohen, E. (1981). Sociology looks at team teaching. *Research in Sociology of Education and Socialization, 2,* 163–193.

Cohen, M. (1983). Instructional, management and social conditions in effective schools. In A. O. Webb & L. D. Webb (Eds.), *School finance and school improvement: Linkages in the 1980's.* Cambridge, MA: Ballinger.

Cohen, M. (1987). Improving school effectiveness: Lessons from research. In V. Richardson-Koehler (Ed.), *Educators' handbook: A research perspective.* New York: Longman.

Coleman, J. S., Campbell, E., Hobson, C., McPartland, J., Mood, A., Weinfield, F., & York, R. (1966). *Equality of educational opportunity.* Washington, DC: U.S. Government Printing Office.

Colton, D. L. (1985). Vision. *National Forum, 65*(2), 33–35.

Cook, G. E. (1988, April). *Patterns of verbal interaction in supervisory feedback conferences.* Paper presented at the annual meeting of the American Educational Research Association, New Orleans.

Copeland, W. D. (1983, April). *Classroom management and student teachers' cognitive abilities: A relationship.* Paper presented at the annual meeting of the American Educational Research Association, Montreal.

Crawford, J. (1983). A study of instructional processes in Title I classes: 1981–82. *Journal of Research and Evaluation of the Oklahoma City Public Schools, 13*(1), 1–25.

Crawford, W. J., King, C. E., Brophy, J. E., & Evertson, C. M. (1975, March). *Error rates and question difficulty related to elementary children's learning.* Paper presented at the annual meeting of the American Educational Research Association, Washington, DC.

Cuban, L. (1983). Effective schools: A friendly but cautionary note. *Phi Delta Kappan, 64,* 695-696.

Cuban, L. (1988, April). *How did teachers teach?* Paper presented at the annual meeting of the American Educational Research Association, New Orleans.

D'Amico, J. (1982). Each effective school may be one of a kind. *Educational Leadership, 40*(3), 61–62.

Davis, G. A. (1986). *Creativity is forever* (2nd ed.). Dubuque, IA: Kendall/Hunt.

Davis, G. A., & Rimm, S. B. (1989). *Education of the gifted and talented* (2nd ed.). Englewood Cliffs, NJ: Prentice Hall.

Deal, T. E. (1987). Effective school principals: Counselors, engineers, pawnbrokers, poets . . . or instructional leaders. In W. D. Greenfield (Ed.), *Instructional leadership: Concepts, issues, and controversies.* Needham Heights, MA: Allyn & Bacon.

Deal, T. E., & Kennedy, A. A. (1982). *Corporate cultures: The rites and rituals of corporate life.* Reading, MA: Addison-Wesley.

DeBevoise, W. (1984). Synthesis of research on the principal as instructional leader. *Educational Leadership, 42*(2), 14–20.

Denham, C., & Lieberman, A. (Eds.). (1980). *Time to learn.* Washington, DC: National Institute of Education.

Denscombe, M. (1985). *Classroom control: A sociological perspective.* London: George, Allen & Unwin.

DeTure, L. R., & Miller, A. P. (1985). *The effects of a written protocol model on teacher acquisition of extended wait-time.* Paper presented at the annual meeting of the National Science Teachers Association, Cincinnati, OH.

Dillon-Peterson, B. (1986). Trusting teachers to know what's good for them. In K. K. Zumwalt (Ed.), *Improving teaching: 1988 ASCD yearbook.* Alexandria, VA: Association for Supervision and Curriculum Development.

Doyle, W. (1985). Classroom organization and management. In M. E. Wittrock (Ed.), *Handbook of research on teaching* (3rd ed.). Chicago: Rand-McNally.

Duke, D. L. (1979). Environmental influences on classroom management. In D. L. Duke (Ed.), *Classroom management* (78th yearbook of the National Society for the Study of Education, Part 2). Chicago, IL: University of Chicago Press.

Dunkin, M., & Biddle, B. (1974). *The study of teaching.* New York: Holt.

Dweck, C. S., & Elliot, E. S. (1983). Achievement motivation. In P. Mussen & E. M. Hetherington (Eds.), *Handbook of child psychology.* New York: Wiley.

Dwyer, D. C. (1984). Forging successful schools: Realistic expectations for principals. *Educational Horizons, 63,* 3–8.

Dwyer, D. C., Lee, G. V., Barnett, B. G., Filby, N. N., & Rowan, B. (1984). *Case studies of the instructional management behavior of principals.* San Francisco: Far West Laboratory for Educational Research and Development.

Dwyer, D. C., Lee, G. V., Rowan, B., & Bossert, S. T. (1982). *The principal's role in instructional management: Five participant observation studies of principals in action.* San Francisco: Far West Laboratory for Educational Research and Development.

Dwyer, D. C., Lee, G. V., Rowan, B., & Bossert, S. T. (1983). *Five principals in action: Perspectives on instructional management.* San Francisco: Far West Laboratory for Educational Research and Development.

Edmonds, R. R. (1978). *A discussion of the literature and issues related to effective schooling.* St. Louis, MO: CEMREL. (ERIC Document Reproduction Service No. ED 142 610)

Edmonds, R. R. (1979). Effective schools for the urban poor. *Educational Leadership, 37,* 15–27.

Edmonds, R. R. (1981). Making public schools effective. *School Policy, 12*(2), 56–60.

Edmonds, R. R. (1982). Programs of school improvement: An overview. *Educational Leadership, 40*(3), 4–11.

Edmonds, R. R. (1983). *Search for effective schools: The identification and analysis of city schools that are instructionally effective for poor children* (Unpublished final report). East Lansing: Michigan State University.

Emmer, E. T. (1987). Classroom management and discipline. In V. Richardson-Koehler (Ed.), *Educators' handbook: A research perspective.* New York: Longman.

Emmer, E. T., & Evertson, C. M. (1981). Synthesis of research on classroom management. *Educational Leadership, 38,* 342–347.

Emmer, E. T., Evertson, C. M., & Anderson, L. (1980). Effective classroom management at the beginning of the school year. *Elementary School Journal, 80,* 219–231.

Emmer, E. T., Evertson, C. M., Sanford, J. P., Clements, B., & Worsham, M. E. (1984). *Classroom management for secondary teachers.* Englewood Cliffs, NJ: Prentice-Hall.

Erickson, F. (1986). Tasks in time: Objects of study in a natural history of teaching. In K. K. Zumwalt (Ed.), *Improving teaching: 1986 ASCD yearbook.* Alexandria, VA: Association for Supervision and Curriculum Development.

Evertson, C. M., Anderson, C., Anderson, L., & Brophy, J. E. (1980). Relationships between classroom behaviors and student outcomes in junior high mathematics and English classes. *American Educational Research Journal, 17,* 43–60.

Evertson, C. M., & Emmer, E. T .(1982). Effective management at the beginning of the school year in junior high classes. *Journal of Educational Psychology, 74,* 485-498.

Evertson, C. M., Emmer, E. T., Clements, B., Sanford, J. P., & Worsham, M. E. (1984). *Classroom management for elementary teachers.* Englewood Cliffs, NJ: Prentice-Hall.

Fetler, M. E., & Carlson, D. C. (1985). Identification of exemplary schools on a large scale. In G. R. Austin & H. Garber (Eds.), *Research on exemplary schools.* New York: Academic Press.

Firestone, W. A., & Herriot, R. E. (1982). Prescriptions for effective elementary schools don't fit secondary schools. *Educational Leadership, 40*(3), 51–53.

Fisher, C., Filby, N., Marliave, R., Cahen, L., Dishaw, M., Moore, J., & Berliner, D. C. (1978). *Teaching behaviors, academic learning time and student achievement: Final report of Phase III-B, Beginning Teacher Evaluation Study.* San Francisco: Far West Laboratory for Educational Research and Development.

Floden, R. E., Porter, A. C., Schmidt, W. H., & Freeman, D. J. (1980). Don't they all measure the same thing? Consequences of standardized test selection. In E. L. Baker & E. S. Quellmalz (Eds.), *Educational testing and evaluation: Design, analysis, and policy.* Beverly Hills, CA: Sage.

Frederickson, J. (1975). *School effectiveness and equality of educational opportunity.* Cambridge, MA: Center for Urban Studies, Harvard University.

Gage, N. L. (1978). *The scientific basis of the art of teaching.* New York: Teachers College Press.

Gage, N. L. (1984). What do we know about teaching effectiveness? *Phi Delta Kappan, 66,* 87-93.

Gage, N. L. (1985). *Hard gains in the soft sciences.* Bloomington, IN: Phi Delta Kappa.

Gage, N. L., & Berliner, D. C. (1984). *Educational psychology* (3rd ed.). Boston: Houghton Mifflin.

Gall, M., Fielding, G., Schalock, D., Charters, W., & Wiczinski, J. (1984). *Involving the principal in teachers' staff development: Effects on the quality of mathematics instruction in elementary schools.* Eugene, OR: Center for Educational Policy and Management, University of Oregon.

Goldhammer, K. (1971). *Elementary school principals and their schools.* Eugene, OR: Center for the Advanced Study of Educational Administration, University of Oregon.

Goldsberry, L. (Discussant). (1988, April). In M. Gall (Chair), *The supervisory conference.* Symposium conducted at the annual meeting of the American Educational Research Association, New Orleans.

Good, T. L. (1983). Classroom research: A decade of progress. *Educational Psychologist, 18*(3), 127–144.

Good, T. L., & Brophy, J. E. (1977). *Educational psychology: A realistic approach* (2nd ed.). New York: Holt.

Good, T. L., & Brophy, J. E. (1985). School effects. In M. E. Wittrock (Ed.), *Handbook of research on teaching* (3rd ed.). Chicago: Rand-McNally.

Good, T. L., & Grouws, D. A. (1979). The Missouri Mathematics Effectiveness Project: An experimental study in fourth grade classrooms. *Journal of Educational Psychology, 71,* 355–361.

Good, T. L., Grouws, D., & Beckerman, T. (1978). Curriculum pacing: Some empirical data in mathematics. *Journal of Curriculum Studies, 10,* 75–81.

Good, T. L., Grouws, D., & Ebmeier, M. (1983). *Active mathematics teaching.* New York: Longman.

Good, T. L., & Weinstein, R. S. (1986). Teacher expectations: A framework for exploring classrooms. In K. K. Zumwalt (Ed.), *Improving teaching: 1986 ASCD yearbook.* Alexandria, VA: Association for Supervision and Curriculum Development.

Goodlad, J. (1983). *A place called school: Prospects for the future.* New York: McGraw-Hill.

Greenfield, W. D. (1987). Moral imagination and interpersonal competence: Antecedents to instructional leadership. In W. D. Greenfield (Ed.), *Instructional leadership: Concepts, issues, and controversies.* Boston: Allyn & Bacon.

Grimmett, P. P., & Crehan, P. (1988, April). *Conferencing strategies used by supervisors of high conceptual level interacting with teachers of low conceptual level and effects on classroom management practices.* Paper presented at the annual meeting of the American Educational Research Association, New Orleans.

Gump, P. V. (1982). School settings and their keeping. In D. L. Duke (Ed.), *Helping teachers manage classrooms.* Alexandria, VA: Association for Supervision and Curriculum Development.

Haggerson, N. (1988, April). *Empowerment in supervision: A case study.* Paper presented at the annual meeting of the American Educational Research Association, New Orleans.

Hall, G. E., Hord, S. M., Huling, L. L., Rutherford, W. L., & Stiegelbauer, S. M. (1983, March). *Leadership variables associated with successful school improvement.* Paper presented at the annual meeting of the American Educational Research Association, Montreal.

Hallinger, P., & Murphy, J. (1987). Instructional leadership in the school context. In W. D. Greenfield (Ed.), *Instructional leadership: Concepts, issues, and controversies.* Boston: Allyn & Bacon.

Hechinger, F. M. (1981). Foreword. In J. M. Lipham, *Effective principal, effective school.* Reston, VA: National Association of Secondary School Principals.

Hiller, J., Fisher, G., & Kaess, W. (1969). A computer investigation of verbal characteristics of effective classroom lecturing. *American Educational Research Journal, 6,* 661–675.

Holland, P. E. (1988). *Implicit assumptions about the supervisory conference: A review and analysis of literature.* Paper presented at the annual meeting of the American Educational Research Association, New Orleans.

Holmes Group. (1986). *Tomorrow's teachers.* East Lansing, MI: Author.

Huberman, M. (1985). What knowledge is of most worth to teachers? A knowledge-use perspective. *Teaching and Teacher Education, 1,* 251–262.

Hunter, M. (1984). Knowing, teaching, and supervising. In P. L. Hosford (Ed.), *Using what we know about teaching.* Alexandria, VA: Association for Supervision and Curriculum Development.

Hunter, M. (1985). What's wrong with Madeline Hunter? *Educational Leadership, 42,*(5), 57–60.

Jencks, C. S., Smith, M. S., Ackland, H., Bane, M. J., Cohen, D., Gintis, H., Heyns, B., & Michelson, S. (1972). *Inequality: A reassessment of family and schooling in America.* New York: Harper & Row.

Jones, N. A. (1980). The effect of type and complexity of teacher questions on student response wait time. *Dissertation Abstracts International, 41*(2), 529–A.

Jones, V., & Jones, L. (1986). *Comprehensive classroom management.* Newton, MA: Allyn & Bacon.

Klitgaard, R. E., & Hall, G. R. (1974). Are there unusually effective schools? *Journal of Human Resources, 10,* 90–106.

Kounin, J. S. (1970). *Discipline and group management in classrooms.* Melbourne, FL: Robert E. Krieger.

Land, M. L. (1979). Low-inference variables and teacher clarity: Effects on student concept learning. *Journal of Educational Psychology, 71,* 795–799.

Lee, G. (1987). Instructional leadership in a junior high school: Managing realities and creating opportunities. In W. D. Greenfield (Ed.), *Instructional leadership: Concepts, issues, and controversies.* Boston: Allyn & Bacon.

Leinhardt, G. (1985, March). *The development of an expert explanation: An analysis of a sequence of subtraction lessons.* Paper presented at the annual meeting of the American Educational Research Association, Chicago.

Leinhardt, G., & Greeno, J. G. (1986). The cognitive skill of teaching. *Journal of Educational Psychology, 78,* 79–85.

Lezotte, L. W., Edmonds, R. R., & Ratner, G. (1974). *A final report: Remedy for school failure to equitably deliver basic school skills.* East Lansing: Department of Urban and Metropolitan Studies, Michigan State University.

Lieberman, A. (1988). Expanding the leadership team. *Educational Leadership, 45*(5), 4–8.

Lipham, J. M. (1981). *Effective principal, effective school.* Reston, VA: National Association of Secondary School Principals.

Lipsitz, J. (1983). *Successful schools for young adolescents.* New Brunswick, NJ: Transaction Press.

Little, J. W. (1981). *School success and staff development: The role of staff development in urban desegregated schools.* Boulder, CO: Center for Action Research.

Little, J. W. (1987). Teachers as colleagues. In V. Richardson-Koehler (Ed.), *Educators' handbook: A research perspective.* New York: Longman.

Little, J. W., & Bird, T. D. (1984). *Report on a pilot study of school-level collegial teaming.* San Francisco: Far West Laboratory for Educational Research and Development.

Little, J. W., & Bird, T. D. (1987). Instructional leadership "close to the classroom" in secondary schools. In W. D. Greenfield (Ed.), *Instructional leadership: Concepts, issues, and controversies.* Boston: Allyn & Bacon.

Mack, D. P. (1988, April). *Policy and operation issues in ESA staff development activities.* Paper presented at the annual meeting of the American Educational Research Association, New Orleans.

Mackenzie, D. E. (1983). Research for school improvement: An appraisal of some recent trends. *Educational Researcher, 12*(4), 5–17.

Manasse, A. L. (1985). Improving conditions for principal effectiveness: Policy implications of research. *Elementary School Journal, 85*(3), 439–463.

Marliave, R., & Filby, J. N. (1986). Success rates: A measure of task appropriateness. In C. W. Fisher & D. C. Berliner (Eds.), *Perspectives on instructional time.* New York: Longman.

Martin, W. J., & Willower, D. J. (1981). The managerial behavior of high school principals. *Educational Administration Quarterly, 17*, 69–90.

McClure, R. M. (1988, April). *Stages and phases of school-based renewal efforts.* Paper presented at the annual meeting of the American Educational Research Association, New Orleans.

McCormack-Larkin, M., & Kritek, W. J. (1983). Milwaukee's project RISE. *Educational Leadership, 40*, 16–21.

McDonald, F. (1976). Report on Phase I of the Beginning Teacher Evaluation Study. *Journal of Teacher Education, 27*(1), 39–42.

McDonald, F., & Elias, P. (1976). *The effects of teaching performance on pupil learning. Beginning Teacher Evaluation Study, Phase II, 1974–1976.* Princeton, NJ: Educational Testing Service.

Michaels, K. (1988). Caution: Second-wave reform taking place. *Educational Leadership, 45*(5), 3.

Miller, J. D. (1983). Scientific literacy: A conceptual and empirical review. *Daedalus, 112*(2), 29–48.

Minneapolis Board of Education. (1981). *Critical choices: The climate for learning in the Minneapolis public schools.* Minneapolis Public Schools Discussion Package No. 8. Minneapolis, MN: Author.

Morine-Dershimer, G., & Beyerbach, B. (1987). Moving right along . . . In V. Richardson-Koehler (Ed.), *Educators' handbook: A research perspective.* New York: Longman.

Morris, V. C., Crowson, R. L., Hurwitz, E., & Porter-Gehrie, C. (1982). The urban principal: Middle manager in the educational bureaucracy. *Phi Delta Kappan, 63,* 689–692.

New York State Department of Education. (1974). *School factors influencing reading achievement: A case study of two inner-city schools.* Albany: State Office of Education.

Odden, A. R. (1988, April). *The PACE study of education reform implementation in California.* Paper presented at the annual meeting of the American Educational Research Association, New Orleans.

Ornstein, A. C. (1969). Techniques and fundamentals for teaching the disadvantaged. In A. C. Ornstein & P. D. Vairo (Eds.), *How to teach the disadvantaged.* New York: McKay.

Peterfreund Associates. (1970). *Innovation and change in public school systems.* Englewood Cliffs, NJ: Author.

Peterson, K. D. (1986). Vision and problem finding in principals' work: Values and cognition in administration. *Peabody Journal of Education, 63,* 87–106.

Peterson, T. (1988, April). *Education reform implementation and impact in South Carolina.* Paper presented at the annual meeting of the American Educational Research Association, New Orleans.

Phi Delta Kappa. (1980). *Why do some urban schools succeed? The Phi Delta Kappa study of exceptional urban elementary schools.* Bloomington, IN: Author.

Purkey, S. C., & Smith, M. S. (1982). Too soon to cheer? Synthesis of research on effective schools. *Educational Leadership, 40*(3), 64–69.

Purkey, S. C., & Smith, M. S. (1983). Effective schools: A review. *Elementary School Journal, 83,* 427–452.

Purkey, W., & Novak, J. (1984). *Inviting school success: A self-concept approach to teaching and learning* (2nd ed.). Belmont, CA: Wadsworth.

Riley, J. P. (1986). The effects of teachers' wait-time and knowledge comprehension questioning on pupil science achievement. *Journal of Research in Science Teaching, 23,* 335–342.

Rodriguez, S., & Johnstone, K. (1986). Staff development through a collegial support group model. In K. K. Zumwalt (Ed.), *Improving teaching: 1986 ASCD yearbook.* Alexandria, VA: Association for Supervision and Curriculum Development.

Rosenshine, B. (1979). Content, time, and direct instruction. In P. L. Peterson & H. L. Walberg (Eds.), *Research on teaching: Concepts, findings, and implications.* Berkeley, CA: McCutchan.

Rosenshine, B. (1986). Synthesis of research on explicit teaching. *Educational Leadership, 43*(7), 60–69.

Rosenshine, B., & Berliner, D. C. (1978). Academic engaged time. *British Journal of Teacher Education, 4,* 3–16.

Rosenthal, R. (1974). *On the social psychology of the self-fulfilling prophecy.* New York: MSS Modular Publications.

Rowan, B. (1984, Summer). Shamanistic rituals in effective schools. *Issues in Education, 2,* 76–87.

Rowan, B., Bossert, S. T., & Dwyer, D. C. (1983). Research on effective schools: A cautionary note. *Educational Researcher, 12*(4), 24–31.

Rowan, B., & Denk, C. E. (1982). *Modelling the academic performance of schools using longitudinal data.* San Francisco: Far West Laboratory for Educational Research and Development.

Rowe, M. B. (1974a). Wait time and rewards as instructional variables, their influence in language, logic and fate control: Part 1. Wait time. *Journal of Research in Science Teaching, 11,* 81–94.

Rowe, M. B. (1974b). Reflections on wait-time: Some methodological questions. *Journal of Research in Science Teaching, 11,* 263-279.

Rowe, M. B. (1974c). Pausing phenomena: Influence on the quality of instruction. *Journal of Psycholinguistics Research, 3,* 203–223.

Rutherford, W. L. (1985). School principals as effective leaders. *Phi Delta Kappan, 67*(1), 31–34.

Rutter, M. (1983). School effects on pupil progress: Research findings and policy implications. In L. S. Shulman & G. Sykes (Eds.), *Handbook of teaching and policy.* New York: Longman.

Rutter, M., Maugham, B., Mortimore, P., Ouston, J., & Smith, A. (1979). *Fifteen thousand hours: Secondary schools and their effects on children.* Cambridge, MA: Harvard University Press.

Sanford, J., Emmer, E. T., & Clements, B. (1983). Improving classroom management. *Educational Leadership, 41,* 56–60.

Schwille, J., Porter, A., Belli, G., Floden, R., Freeman, D., Knappen, L., Kuhs, T., & Schmidt, W. (1983). Teachers as policy brokers in the content of elementary school mathematics. In L. S. Shulman and G. Sykes (Eds.), *Handbook of teaching and policy.* New York: Longman.

Sergiovanni, T. J. (1987). *The principalship: A reflective practice perspective.* Boston: Allyn & Bacon.

Shapiro, S. (1975). Preschool ecology: A study of three environmental variables. *Reading Improvement, 12,* 236–241.

Shavelson, R. J. (1983). Review of research on teachers' pedagogical judgments, plans, and decisions. *Elementary School Journal, 83,* 392–414.

Shrum, J. L. (1985). Wait time and student performance level in second language classrooms. *Journal of Classroom Interaction, 20*(1), 29–35.

Silverstein, J. M. (1979). *Individual and environmental correlates of pupil problematic and nonproblematic classroom behavior.* Unpublished doctoral dissertation, New York University.

Sirotnik, K. A. (1985). School effectiveness: A Bandwagon in search of a tune. *Educational Administration Quarterly, 21*(2), 135–140.

Sizer, T. R. (1985). Common sense. *Educational Leadership, 42*(6), 21–22.

Smith, L. C., & Geoffrey, W. (1968). *The complexities of an urban classroom.* New York: Holt, Rinehart & Winston.

Smith, L. R. (1977). Aspects of teacher discourse and student achievement in mathematics. *Journal for Research in Mathematics Education, 8,* 194–204.

Smith, L. R., & Land, M. L. (1981). Low-inference verbal behaviors related to teacher clarity. *Journal of Classroom Interaction, 17,* 37–42.

Smith, M., & Glass, G. (1980). Meta-analysis of research on class size and its relationship to attitudes and instruction. *American Educational Research Journal, 17*, 419–433.

Squires, D. A., Huitt, W. G., & Segars, J. K. (1983). *Effective schools and classrooms.* Alexandria, VA: Association for Supervision and Curriculum Development.

Stallings, J. A. (1986). Using time effectively: A self-analytic approach. In K. K. Zumwalt (Ed.), *Improving teaching: 1986 ASCD yearbook.* Alexandria, VA: Association for Supervision and Curriculum Development.

Stallings, J. A., & Kaskowitz, D. (1974). *Follow through classroom observation evaluation, 1972–1973.* Menlo Park, CA: Stanford Research Institute.

Stallings, J. A., Cory, R., Fairweather, J., & Needels, M. (1977). *Early childhood education classroom evaluation.* Menlo Park, CA: Stanford Research Institute.

Stallings, J. A., Cory, R., Fairweather, J., & Needels, M. (1978). *A study of basic reading skills taught in secondary schools.* Menlo Park, CA: Stanford Research Institute.

Stephans, E. R. (1988, April). *Nine-state study of ESA staff development activities.* Paper presented at the annual meeting of the American Educational Research Association, New Orleans.

Stodolsky, S. S., Ferguson, T. L., & Wimpelberg, K. (1981). The recitation persists, but what does it look like? *Journal of Curriculum Studies, 13*, 121–130.

Swift, J. N., & Gooding, C. T. (1983). Interaction of wait time feedback and questioning instruction on middle school science teaching. *Journal of Research in Science Teaching, 20*, 721–730.

Sykes, G. (1983). Contradictions, ironies and promises unfulfilled: The need for screens and the status of teaching. *Phi Delta Kappan, 65*, 87–9.

Thornbury, R. (Ed.). (1974). *Teachers' centres.* New York: Agathon Press.

Tobin, K. (1986). Effects of teacher wait time on discourse characteristics in mathematics and language arts classes. *American Educational Research Journal, 23*, 191–200.

Tobin, K. (1987). The role of wait time in higher cognitive level learning. *Review of Educational Research, 57*, 69–95.

Tobin, K., & Capie, W. (1982). Relationships between classroom process variables and middle school science achievement. *Journal of Educational Psychology, 14*, 441-454.

Ubben, G. C., & Hughes, L. W. (1987). *The principal: Creative leadership for effective schools.* Newton, MA: Allyn & Bacon.

U.S. Department of Education. (1986). *What works: Research about teaching and learning.* Washington, DC: Author.

U.S. Department of Education. (1987). *What works: Research about teaching and learning* (2nd ed.). Washington, DC: Author.

Van Der Burg, K. (1986). *Effective school characteristics: A comparison of expert and parent perspectives.* Unpublished doctoral dissertation, University of Wisconsin, Madison.

Walberg, H. J. (1984). Improving the productivity of America's schools. *Educational Leadership, 41*(8), 19–27.

Walberg, H. J. (1985). Syntheses of research on teaching. In M. C. Wittrock (Ed.), *Handbook of research on teaching* (3rd ed.). Chicago: Rand-McNally.

Walter, J. E., & Stanfield, P. (1988, April). *Organizational environments and effective schooling.* Paper presented at the annual meeting of the American Educational Research Association, New Orleans.

Weber, G. (1971). *Inner-city children can be taught to read: Four successful schools.* Washington, DC: Council for Basic Education.

Webster, W. J. (1988, April). *An effective educational intervention: The center concept.* Paper presented at the annual meeting of the American Educational Research Association, New Orleans.

Weinstein, C. S. (1979). The physical environment of the school: A review of the research. *Review of Educational Research, 49,* 557–610.

Willower, D. J., & Kmetz, J. T. (1982, April). *The managerial behavior of elementary school principals.* Paper presented at the annual meeting of the American Educational Research Association, New York.

Willms, J. D., & Raudenbush, S. W. (1988, April). *The stability of school effects.* Paper presented at the annual meeting of the American Educational Research Association, New Orleans.

Wynne, E. A. (1981). Looking at good schools. *Phi Delta Kappan, 62,* 337–382.

Yinger, R. J. (1977). *A study of teacher planning: Description and theory development using ethnographic and information processing methods.* Unpublished doctoral dissertation, Michigan State University, East Lansing.

Index